Climate Solutions Beyond Capitalism

LIBERATION MEDIA

SAN FRANCISCO

ISBN: 978-0-9910303-6-1
Library of Congress Control Number: 2020934000
Cover illustration: Mitch Malloy

Written by

Tina Landis

Foreword by

Jodi Dean

Edited by

Jane Cutter

Staff

Jiyoon Ahn, Nic de la Riva, Lo Ferris, Saul Kanowitz, Rosa Laurel,
Beth Massey, Nathaniel McGuigan, Susan Muysenburg, Keith Pavlik

Liberation Media

2969 Mission Street #201
San Francisco, CA 94110
(415) 821-6171
books@LiberationMedia.org
www.LiberationMedia.org

Climate Solutions Beyond Capitalism

Foreword

BY JODI DEAN

EVERY day we hear about how bad the climate crisis is: raging fires, rising tides, melting permafrost, warming oceans and dying species. This publication confronts the negative and individualizing message of the capitalist class with revolutionary optimism.

Sometimes we are advised about what we can do as individuals to combat climate change: switch to different lightbulbs or eat less meat or walk to work. Given the enormous scale of the bad, it is hard to take this advice seriously. Most of us live too far away from our waged jobs to make walking feasible, and everybody knows how poor public transportation is in the United States. Likewise, people have switched lightbulbs and altered their diets, and still our planet's air, land and seas are getting warmer. The fossil fuel sector continues to expand; emissions continue to increase; the amount of carbon in the atmosphere continues to grow.

The inadequate and individualized advice goes hand in hand with the gloom and doom: The ruling class does not want people to think that collectively we can change the world. The capitalists would rather have us focus on our individual choices, wants and fears. This is because the capitalist system can only persist so long as most of us think changing it is impossible — but it is not.

We can respond to climate change in a way that will save human and nonhuman lives, enhance community well-being and strengthen working-class power. We can respond by fighting for and building socialism. As stated in the program of the Party for Socialism and Liberation, "For the people and planet to live, capitalism must go."

IT IS NOT ABOUT CLIMATE DENIAL ANYMORE

"Climate Solutions Beyond Capitalism" begins with the key insight that the primary struggle around climate change is not against denial. The climate denial ship has sunk. Other than a few fringe elements, virtually all of the establishment accepts the reality of climate change. Nearly every oil and gas company acknowledge that carbon emissions contribute to global warming. It is widely accepted that the energy sector is responsible for roughly 70 percent of global emissions. One hundred and thirty banks have adopted United Nations climate principles. These banks include Citigroup, Deutsche Bank and Barclays. The U.S. military treats climate change as a major security threat. It is actively planning for the likely escalation of political unrest as millions are forced to migrate because their homelands have become unlivable. Despite what President Donald Trump says, and despite what we might hear from cranky relatives, climate change is a fact. Oil and gas companies, banks and the U.S. military, that is, key sectors of capitalist class power, are preparing for the climate crisis, hoping to use the crisis to expand their power.

The U.S. military treats climate change as a major security threat. It is actively planning for the likely escalation of political unrest as millions are forced to migrate because their homelands have become unlivable.

Consider, for example, how financial analysts study climate change in order to advise investors and corporations on how to respond to and profit from the warming climate. A recent financial industry report noted that the fossil fuel sector emitted as much greenhouse gas in the 28 years since the official acknowledgement of global warming as it had in the previous 237 years. Facing the reality of climate change, the fossil fuel sector doubled down, drilling more wells and laying more pipeline as fast as it could before people developed the political will to stop them.

It is also the case that the U.S. mainstream has started to recognize the role of capitalism in climate change. We see this recognition in analyses that point out the impact of the rise of industrialism on the amount of carbon dioxide in the atmosphere. We see it in criticisms of the commodity-oriented consumer lifestyle. We even see it in criticisms of developing countries who continue to rely on coal: Most news articles focus on consumption, not on commodity production for the sake of private profit — the real site of the problem.

Students lead a die-in at Chicago's Millennium Park during the Dec. 6, 2019 Climate Strike.

The issue we face, then, is not climate denial. It is not even denial of capitalism's role in the climate crisis. The issue is how to respond to the crisis. Should we maintain the system that is driving the crisis or create a new, better and more sustainable system? This publication argues that we should create a new one — and shows us how it is possible.

CAPITALISM IS THE PROBLEM

The ruling class does not want to see any response to the climate crisis that impinges on their wealth and power. We saw the impact of this position in the failure of the 2019 United Nations Climate Change Conference in Madrid, the important climate conference that was supposed to formalize rules for implementing the Paris climate agreement reached in 2015. Rich countries, in particular the United States and Australia, refused to commit to helping developing nations adapt to the changing climate. They also remained attached to the old and unworkable carbon credit plan part of the Kyoto accord.

More generally, capitalists think that the free market is already addressing the climate crisis. For example they point to natural gas, nuclear energy and expensive and futuristic technologies for sucking carbon out of the atmosphere. None of these responses do anything but buttress the capitalist system and deflect attention from the work that needs to be done. Natural gas — championed by Barack Obama as a bridge fuel — has driven the fracking revolution. Not only does methane have greater warming properties than carbon, but natural gas has been the key to the U.S. strategy for becoming a net fossil fuel exporter, that is, for U.S. energy dominance and imperial power. Nuclear plants take decades to build. Their radioactive waste cannot be safely stored or disposed of — and Native people have been some of the primary victims of the nuclear energy's storage of hazardous waste on their sacred lands. The risk of meltdowns makes nuclear plants extraordinarily dangerous, as we learned most recently when a tidal wave struck Fukushima, Japan in 2011. High-tech machines for carbon capture have not yet been built in a form that can scale. At this point, they are expensive to build and require a lot of energy to run. Capitalists want us to think that capitalism is adaptable and responsive enough to develop what is needed to adapt to the changing climate. What history shows is that capitalism's orientation toward profits means that it will exploit workers and the environment, squeezing the life out of both for the sake of more money. Capitalists have hidden the evidence of the damage caused by fossil fuels. They offload the poisonous byproducts of their industry onto poor communities, disproportionately those of people of color. Capitalism is not oriented toward justice and meeting the needs of the many. It cannot solve the problems that accompany climate change.

> What history shows is that capitalism's orientation toward profits means that it will exploit workers and the environment, squeezing the life out of both for the sake of more money.

Capitalists today are also deeply worried that climate change might be "the death knell of economic freedom" as the Economist magazine fretted in its special issue on the climate. Capitalists are right to worry. Most of us know full well that when it comes to profits, capitalists are oriented toward competition, not cooperation. They cheat and outdo each other in the race for larger shares of the market and higher profits. They certainly are not concerned with improving the lives of workers. The system operates to keep wages down and profits high. It is no wonder, then, that the climate movement has come to embrace climate justice — the fight against a climate apartheid that sacrifices poor and working people and a fight for a just transition. No equitable response to the climate crisis can be built on the backs of the working class and at the cost of the lives of frontline and fence line communities. Markets cannot deliver a just transition because markets chew people up and spit them out, leaving them impoverished and unemployed.

SOCIALISM IS THE SOLUTION

This pamphlet rejects the capitalist fiction that it could ever provide a just response to the climate crisis. It demonstrates why we need a planned economy and provides concrete examples of a collective and sustainable approach to agriculture, land use, the oceans and renewable energy.

Socialism is the solution to climate change because climate change is class struggle. Climate change has not been caused by everyone. Not everyone has benefitted from industrialization. We see this most clearly at the international level. The largest carbon emitters — which include the United States and the European Union — are responsible for the largest percentage of carbon emissions. The climate crisis is not the fault of the smaller, developing countries which have long been exploited by colonial and imperial powers like the United States. It is also not the fault of the poor, who globally are disproportionately women and people of color. The top 1 percent are responsible for 175 times more emissions than the bottom 10 percent. And yet those in the bottom 10 percent are the ones already feeling the impact of the crisis as they are forced to migrate, confront decreasing agricultural yields and suffer from fires, floods, storms and heat waves.

Saving the planet or, more precisely, ensuring that the earth remains livable for the majority of people and species, requires dismantling the U.S. war machine. The U.S. military is the largest institutional emitter of warming gases on the planet. Its bases, occupations, coups and illegal wars amplify the destabilizing effects of the warming climate. This tells us that the struggle for a just response to the climate crisis is also a struggle for peace. At a time when the world needs to come together to develop a collective response, U.S. imperialism is a major obstacle. We must build the socialist power necessary to remove it.

Because climate change is class struggle, a struggle against imperialism and a matter of relations of production, local solutions are not enough. The response to climate change has to be big enough to take on enormous corporations and the entire capitalist class, and win. Our task is to build a collective power capable of seizing the state. This will allow us to nationalize the corporations, reign in and dismantle the military as an imperialist force, build new electrical grids, change the transportation system and reorganize life and work. Ending U.S. imperialism will be a major step toward building the international trust necessary for global cooperation. It will also let us get to work in providing the material reparations and support long overdue to colonized peoples and victims of U.S. aggression.

Responding to the climate crisis is not a matter of individual morality and consumer choices. The individualizing focus on personal lifestyle choices is one of the ways capitalism tries to divert attention from the system as a whole. Instead of joining together to fight against a system that pursues profit over people, people turn on each other, chastising one another for consumer choices in a context where we are all dependent on consumer items for meeting our basic needs. What has to change is what is produced and how it is produced. This will only change when the basic relations of production, work and ownership change. And this requires socialist revolution. □

Preface

The crisis from a socialist perspective

F you read the mainstream media, you may get the sense that our extinction is inevitable or that the solutions are just too impractical to implement. Studies show that 98 percent of news stories on climate change cover only the negative effects,[1] omitting all the work being done on adaptive solutions in communities and laboratories around the world. U.S. mainstream media outlets are controlled by just six companies and represent the viewpoint of the ruling class — which wants to maintain "business as usual" so they can continue to enrich themselves. If the population is not aware that there are solutions, they are less likely to demand action.[2]

The establishment never directs the blame for the crisis on the capitalist system itself. They like to pretend that no other economic system has ever or will ever exist. Instead, they promote piecemeal voluntary solutions that place the burden on individuals and are often out of reach to the majority of the population that is struggling to live paycheck to paycheck. While individuals can choose to consume less and conserve more, this does little to affect the overall output of greenhouse gas emissions. Individual behavior change does not alter the production model, which creates the vast majority of waste, pollution and environmental degradation far beyond the control of individuals. Just 100 companies have been the source of 71 percent of emissions since 1988.[3]

While recycling, consuming less animal products, driving and flying less and buying sustainable local products is good for the planet, this is not enough. The crisis is global. We need to leave fossil fuels in the ground and immediately expand renewable energy infrastructure. We need to produce only what is needed and provide

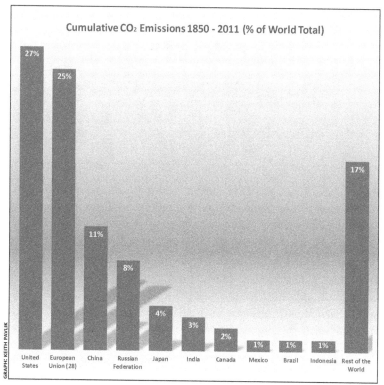

*Industrialized capitalist countries are
the largest contributors to the climate crisis.*

job training in fields that build a sustainable world. We must look to systemic change for solutions.

This publication provides a different perspective from the corporate media narrative. It is not meant to be an all-encompassing scientific paper. Science, like the political landscape, is ever changing. By the time you are reading this publication, there may be new scientific discoveries of solutions or a renewed connection to the indigenous wisdom of ecology. While some solutions today may seem like the best path forward, future research may find new paths that supersede what we know now. The message of this publication is that there are very promising solutions, today and in our future, none of which can or will be implemented in any comprehensive and meaningful way under capitalism, where the law of profit holds progress back.

This publication is meant to be a tool for activists to give an informed and educated voice to counter the demoralization campaign of the ruling class, to look beyond the dead-end solutions within the framework of capitalism, lay out some promising solutions to the climate crisis and paint a picture of the eco-socialist future. It is an urgent call to action to transform the inhumane, unsustainable capitalist system and take an evolutionary leap forward in the way we live and interact with each other and the natural world.

For the majority of our existence, humans survived and advanced due to cooperation. Earth's ecosystems are made up of species living synergistically, providing complementary services to the whole.

As of this writing, record heat waves are scorching the northern hemisphere, while unprecedented wildfires rage across the Arctic region, and catastrophic floods engulf South Asia. Climate change is here and much that has been set into motion cannot be undone. But we can minimize the magnitude of the change by not continuing to add to the problem, as well as by restoring ecosystems, restructuring the system of production and creating resilient communities that can better cope with the effects.[4]

The climate crisis is truly the greatest existential threat humanity has ever faced. The arguments against comprehensive action range from human nature as one of competition and greed to spreading lies about the validity of scientific reports. All serve to uphold the status quo and drive life on Earth to extinction in the service of short-term profits for a few.

For the majority of our existence, humans survived and advanced due to cooperation. Earth's ecosystems are made up of species living synergistically, providing complementary services to the whole. The rise of capitalism and private land ownership ruptured this complementary relation with the ecosystem through the exploitation of nature and workers for commodity production. Modern technology along with a return to ecological practices may allow us to renew our intrinsic relationship with the Earth and provide for the needs of all. But achieving this transformation requires an uprooting of the capitalist system. We can no longer survive as a species under the laws of capitalism, that dictate what can and cannot be achieved based on profitability. In order to maintain a livable planet, we must do away with the system that upholds the needs of corporations above people and the environment.

It is all possible. The technology exists to meet worldwide energy needs with wind, water and solar; to shift to regenerative agricultural practices and feed the world; to restore natural habitats that capture carbon and improve soil health and water resources. We can create egalitarian societies where everyone has equal access to housing, education, jobs, culture and recreation. It will take work. It will take cooperation. It will take the wealthier nations sharing resources and technologies with the Global South as reparations for centuries of colonial and neocolonial plunder. But it can be done.

This publication covers the urgent problems we face and how the capitalist system, by its very nature, is a barrier to a sustainable world, and provides examples of some inspiring current and developing solutions that can be implemented on a mass scale within the framework of an eco-socialist society.

This publication embraces the concept of revolutionary optimism — that we have the tools and insight to change course and that the capitalist system cannot hold back the will of the masses and the evolution of society. The sparks of change may seem small and scattered, but a broad view shows a growing trend emerging worldwide, based on a desire for a new path forward — from a renewed interest in socialism, to breakthroughs in research and technology, to an embrace of traditional indigenous practices that align with nature, to the global youth-led climate movement.

This publication is an urgent call to action and at the same time a call for humility. We must have a sobering look at what industrialization and capitalist development have done to the planet and redefine our relationship with the Earth.

In my years of study, writing and working in the field of climate protection, I have frequently felt despair and grief over what we are losing. Author and journalist Dahr Jamail, who has written on climate for the past decade, shares an important perspective on how he remains steadfast: "Each time another scientific study is released showing yet another acceleration of the loss of ice atop the Arctic Ocean, or sea level rise projections are stepped up yet again, or news of another species that has gone extinct is announced, my heart breaks for what we have done and are doing to the planet. I grieve, yet this ongoing process has become more like peeling back the layers of an onion — there is always more work to do as the crisis we have created for ourselves continues to unfold."[5]

We face an uncertain future. Yet, we cannot foresee what effect our collective actions today will have on the future and the role they will play in the revolutionary transformation of society. It is our duty to step up and do what we can, despite the uncertainty of the outcome — not just for ourselves, but for future generations and all life on the planet. We each have something to contribute — from conversations with co-workers, to organizing in our communities, to supporting organizations taking action, to educating ourselves on the issues, to opening our minds to the possibility of a different way of living in alignment with nature, to building revolutionary socialist organizations. Everyone has something to contribute no matter how small — and the time is now. ☐

Climate Solutions Beyond Capitalism

Chapter 1

Is there a future worth fighting for?

WE are already witnessing unprecedented changes around the globe that make for an uncertain future. At the same time, scientists and engineers are finding solutions that can help minimize the magnitude of the change — with the mission of limiting the rise in global temperatures to 1.5 C above pre-industrial levels rather than the disastrous 4 or 5 C as currently projected — and to mitigate the effects as they unfold. How exactly the changing climate will affect the planet is uncertain. The interactions of the Earth's systems are incredibly complex. It is nearly impossible to model all the feedback scenarios that may occur — one change triggers another, which then creates more warming and more change, and so on. Scientists do not fully understand the interplay of all the natural forces in a stable climate, much less in an unstable one.

The very nature of capitalism creates barriers to funding research and implementation of solutions. Most research funding goes to short-term highly specialized projects where corporations and academic institutions foresee potential profits as the outcome. The profit system upholds intellectual property rights and patents above the needs of society and impedes progress when humanity would be best served by sharing knowledge and research globally to overcome the crisis.

Solutions under capitalism focus on market-based carbon trading schemes, incremental policy changes and technological fixes that aim to make a profit along the way with great risks that outweigh the benefits.

For instance, carbon capture technology — if implemented on the large scale to be effective — would actually increase carbon dioxide emissions beyond its capture capacity due to increased steel

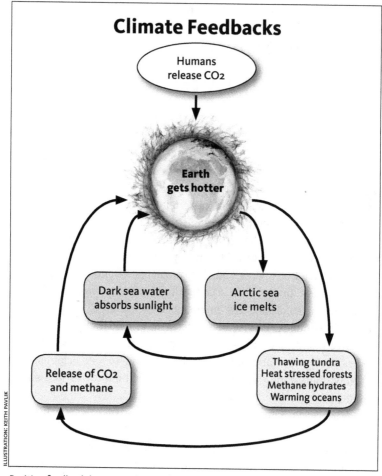

Positive feedback loops accelerate climate change.

production to build these facilities and the energy needed to run them.[1] Such "quick fix" solutions attempt to solve the problem within the for-profit capitalist system while maintaining its unfettered production and resource consumption. This ignores the essence of the problem — humanity's relationship with the natural world.

The time for incremental market-based solutions is over. Cap-and-trade and carbon taxes have done nothing significant to drive down emissions in the long run. Since the problem of climate change was first brought to the world's attention in the 1950's,

Socialist production in the former Soviet Union was planned; only what was needed was produced, preventing the waste of a capitalist consumer economy.

no binding agreement has come from any of the global climate summits. Why is this?

The answer is twofold. Implementation of the systemic change needed requires that we not exceed the carrying capacity of the planet. In other words, only producing what we need, eliminating emissions and waste and limiting resource extraction to what is sustainable in the long term. This means that the capitalist system that bases production goals on the whims of the market, rather than the needs of society, must end. It is an enormously wasteful system where maximizing quarterly returns takes priority over a livable planet.

To solve the crisis, we need a planned economy where resources go to things that benefit society and the planet simultaneously. Such a society is not utopian. We can see glimpses in past socialist revolutions, regardless of their flaws and their challenges of scarcity, which were due to these countries' stage in development, not inherent to the system of socialism. Great achievements were made in these revolutions to overcome famine, illiteracy, inequality and lack of health care and infrastructure. Through a planned economy and the power to steer the resources of society toward a common goal, what had been impossible prior to these revolutions became reality.

The eco-socialist future can be an improvement in the lives of billions of people even within a changing climate, but we must act now. Everyone able to work will have a productive role in making society run. There will be no unemployment or homelessness because housing and a job will be a right, rather than a commodity or something to compete for. There will need to be an expansion of the workforce in many areas — to set up the renewable energy infrastructure, to restore ecosystems, to revolutionize agricultural practices to be local and regenerative, to rebuild cities and towns to be walkable and bikeable eco-cities, and to implement relocation of populations vulnerable to rising seas. We need more doctors, nurses and educators, and more scientists and engineers to find solutions as the crisis unfolds.

Billions of workers worldwide will have opportunities for skilled jobs that are valuable to society unlike current-day employment that often adds no value other than the enrichment of the ruling class. There will be no more need for advertising and production of useless goods. The military-industrial complex and the Pentagon — the biggest unregulated polluter on the planet[2] — will be dismantled. The prison-industrial complex will be eliminated and replaced with rehabilitation and job training programs. The parasitic insurance industry will be abolished and those workers retrained in fields that benefit society. Likewise, workers in extractive industries will be retrained and redeployed in environmentally-sustainable fields. Culture and the arts will be supported and recreation will be a right for all.

What is manufactured will be made to last. Automation will be used to benefit society and we will all work less, unlike under capitalism where it signals destitution for large sectors of the labor force that are no longer needed.

All these possibilities and more can be realized by humanity — and the vast majority want this change. This type of collaborative eco-socialist society is our only chance at surviving the effects of climate change. This is a future worth fighting for. □

Chapter 2

Agriculture and land use

THE path forward requires ecological solutions as well as an immediate decarbonization of our economy. Western methods in the field of ecology, like western medicine, traditionally have focused on the function of a specific part rather than the interactions and contributions of the individual within the whole. To restore the ecological system as a carbon capture and oxygen-producing mechanism for the planet, we need to shift our perspective to the holistic health of the ecosystem.

Despite the fact that many solutions are tied to the restoration of ecosystems, funding and attention are most often given to corporate ventures in carbon capture technology that distract from the enormity of the problem and leave the current system of production unchallenged.

A recent study led by ecologist and geographer Jean-Francois Bastin showed that an extremely effective method to combat climate change is the reforestation of previously forested lands. If 1.9 billion hectares (4.7 billion acres) on five continents were reforested with native species, these forests, once mature, could store two-thirds of all the carbon emitted since the Industrial Revolution.[1]

An immediate ban on fossil fuel combustion would not address the carbon dioxide already in our atmosphere, which has a lifespan of 100 to 150 years and will continue to contribute to climate disruption. Restoration and protection of forests would be the most beneficial tool for carbon capture along with restoration of coastal mangroves, salt marshes and sea grass beds, which store carbon at a rate 40 percent higher than tropical forests. Peat lands store more carbon than all the world's vegetation combined[2] and when kept intact prevent immense amounts of embedded carbon from being released.[3] Targeted by the biofuel industry, a single hectare (2.471 acres) of Indonesian peatland

Restoration of native forests utilizes natural carbon capture mechanisms while increasing biodiversity and cooling the climate.

rainforest releases up to 6,000 tons of carbon dioxide when destroyed to make way for palm oil plantations.[4]

REBALANCING THE BIOSPHERE

The ecological system over millennia has kept a natural balance between different species of flora and fauna, and this balance has been thrown off by humans in just a few centuries. Restoration of these interconnected relationships is one half of the equation of our survival.

Each species acts as a cog in the ecosystem factory. When too many cogs are lost, the factory can no longer produce what all species need for survival, i.e., fresh water, oxygen to breathe and soil nutrients to feed plants. We are now in the midst of the sixth mass extinction with reports of tens of thousands of species being lost annually and nearly 75 percent lost in the insect population.[5] The previous five mass extinctions saw 50 to 90 percent species loss and were triggered by natural disasters such as volcanic eruptions and asteroid strikes. And that's the good news! The sixth is human-caused and largely due to habitat loss and fragmentation from deforestation due to logging, development and agriculture. Since humans are causing it, we can potentially reverse the pressures on species by eliminating the land use changes and restoring habitats. But the changing climate is also a pressure on species.[6]

Over the last 20,000 years of human existence, incremental changes in the climate occurred over long periods of time.[7] The great threat in the current epoch is the extremely fast rate of warming. Instead of having millennia to adapt to minor warming and cooling of the atmosphere, species are now faced with major shifts within decades — far faster than most evolutionary cycles can keep up with. Pressures on species from the warming planet on top of habitat loss from land use change are contributing to the accelerating extinction rates we see today. While many species may be lost, effort and attention to ecosystem restoration along with immediate decarbonization and resource conservation can help ecosystems recover over time so they can continue to provide life-giving resources for the planet.

Native wildlife plays a key balancing role. Protecting and reintroducing native animal populations can aid reforestation by these animals spreading seeds as they roam, and can aid in wildfire prevention by keeping dry undergrowth from building up. In other cases, predators such as wolves play a role by lowering herbivore populations and keeping carbon-sequestering plant life intact.[8]

Research by the Zimovs, a father-son team of scientists working in the Mammoth Steppe in Siberia, has found that reestablishing large native grazing herds protects permafrost from melting. Large herds were lost over thousands of years due to hunting. As the herds dis-

Pleistocene Park, Siberia

PHOTO: PLEISTOCENE PARK FOUNDATION

appeared, grasses that they fed on were replaced by trees and brush. Trees absorb more heat from the sun than snow-covered grasses, resulting in increased soil temperatures and melting permafrost as the climate warms. Additionally, grazers push away snow as they forage, exposing the permafrost to the air, which keeps it 3 F to 4 F cooler without the insulating snow cover. Reintroducing large herds along with tree removal would bring back the grasses and help cool the permafrost. The project, called the Pleistocene Park, has already imported grazing populations from other parts of Russia, Alaska and Canada and has utilized an old Soviet tank to crush the larch, birch and brambles to expose grassy layers below.[9]

Destruction of ecosystems has repercussions beyond just carbon capture capacity and species loss. Deforestation has been linked to the rise of diseases such as dengue, yellow fever, Rocky Mountain spotted fever and Lyme disease that greatly impact public health globally.[10]

Mycelium — whose fruit are mushrooms — are the cornerstone of healthy ecosystems and can also provide medicinal and pest control benefits, remove toxins and radiation from soil and water and potentially serve as a rapidly renewing biofuel source. Mycologist Paul Stamets has conducted studies showing how different species of mycelium ward off carpenter ants, while others attack malaria-carrying mosquito populations. Mycelium introduced into various toxic sites with heavy metals, radioactive materials, fertilizers, munitions or endocrine-disruptors have cleaned the soil and returned them to productive lands within weeks. Similarly, mycelium introduced at the source of agricultural run-off removes bacteria and toxins from the water. Mycelium can detoxify land in a much shorter time frame and can lower costs compared to other bioremediation practices.[11]

Studies in old-growth forests have shown vast communications networks between tree roots and mycelium that work together to share resources, ward off pests and keep the whole ecosystem healthy. The short-sighted forestry practice of growing trees like crops destroys the mycelium network and the soil nutrients through repeated harvesting, a lack of species diversity and introduction of fungicides and herbicides between plantings.[12]

Reforestation restores ecosystems and the carbon capture capacity of degraded lands. A process called the Miyawaki Method

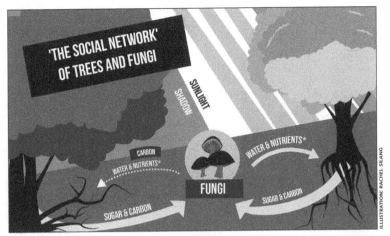

'THE SOCIAL NETWORK' OF TREES AND FUNGI

SUNLIGHT
SHADOW
CARBON
WATER & NUTRIENTS*
WATER & NUTRIENTS*
FUNGI
SUGAR & CARBON
SUGAR & CARBON

ILLUSTRATION: RACHEL SILANG

The mycelium network, which acts as a communication and distribution system for the forest, sends warning of pests and disease, and nutrients to those in need.

has demonstrated immense benefits with little input required, where a dozen native species and other indigenous flora are planted closely together. After just three years, the area becomes self-sustaining as the natural selection of native plants results in a biodiverse, resilient forest. Even the conversion of small plots of land at very low cost can provide the additional benefits of food and medicine for local communities, and act as flood and drought protection.[13]

FOOD PRODUCTION

Agriculture has a major impact on the global ecosystem. To feed the world in the midst of the changing climate, we must shift our land use and agricultural practices to align with the planet's capacity. It means taking a step back from harmful industrial methods that disregard long-term productivity and the health of people and the planet.

Monoculture agriculture is already being challenged by the changing climate with shifting temperatures and rainfall bringing new pests and lower crop yields.[14]

The so-called "Green Revolution" of the 1950s and 1960s replaced traditional agricultural practices with chemical fertilizers, pesticides and mechanization and gave rise to the agribusiness industry we know today.[15] The benefit of increased crop yields came at the cost of depleted

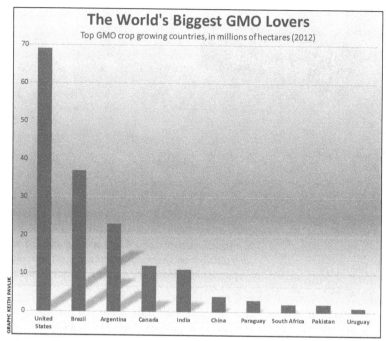

The World's Biggest GMO Lovers
Top GMO crop growing countries, in millions of hectares (2012)

GRAPH: KEITH PAVLIK

Genetically-modified organisms ignore the long-term effects on human health and the ecosystem.

and poisoned soil and groundwater, a 75 percent decline in insect populations and increasing cancer rates, particularly in farming communities. Factory farms have brought about inhumane and unhealthy animal husbandry practices that employ immense amounts of antibiotics and growth hormones and leave behind toxic lagoons of animal waste that often pollute groundwater — all to the detriment of public health.

The myth that we cannot feed the world's people without industrialized agriculture and genetically modified organisms is merely a cover by big agribusiness that enables them to make massive profits at the expense of human health and the planet. Hunger is an issue of distribution, storage and access, not the lack of productive capacity. Under capitalism, food shortages occur due to profit-making schemes like the diversion of food crops to biofuel — a quick fix solution that ignores the negative effects on food access and the ecosystem.[16]

Industrial agricultural practices and immense amounts of food waste (30 to 50 percent of food produced in the United States is discarded), as well as the excessive amount of animal products consumed in the U.S. diet are the true problem. A shift in agriculture to locally-produced, regenerative practices that eliminate long-distance shipping and long-term storage, lower meat consumption and reduced food waste are the key to a low-carbon food production system.

Desertification — which is increasing with the warming climate — is directly linked to the overgrazing of lands as well as deforestation, which can be reversed or prevented through regenerative farming methods and habitat protection.[17]

Returning to indigenous practices that work with the local ecology rather than the capitalist method of exploiting the natural world can rebalance and heal the ecosystem to the benefit of all.

Traditional indigenous home gardens employ agroforestry methods, also known as silvopasture,[18] that incorporate trees with crop production and livestock, protect the land from erosion, recycle nutrients and create resilience to climate impacts. In a warming world with increasing droughts and storms, trees provide beneficial shade and wind protection for crops and help to retain soil moisture. The resulting high productivity meets local needs and avoids the need to transport food, decreasing waste and energy use. This technique has been implemented by farmers in the dry Sahel region of Africa and has resulted in a rise of water tables over the last few decades.[19]

Agroforestry is not merely sustainable but regenerative, meaning it adds to the health and productivity of the ecosystem over time, working with the highly productive mechanisms inherent in forests.

Comprehensive implementation of regenerative agricultural practices best suited for specific regional needs can play a highly beneficial role in slowing global warming and increasing biodiversity.

In 1982 in Brazil, agroecologist Ernst Götsch turned 500 acres of desertified unproductive land that had been clear-cut and left devoid of life into a thriving agroforest. The area now has fertile soil, water running in streams even during the dry season and has seen temperatures drop and rain increase due to the highly productive nature of the restored environment. All of this was achieved without fertilizer or irrigation, but rather in collaboration with natural processes.

Götsch systematized and mechanized his syntropic agriculture techniques so that they can be implemented anywhere regardless of

PHOTO: MARC LEIBER

Syntropic agricultural site in Brazil

climate, soil or acreage. Götsch promotes reconnecting with natural systems as the path forward, saying, "Humans could reconcile themselves with the planet, finding a way to be useful and welcomed in the system. But we don't realize that, we can't see because we have disconnected ourselves from life on the planet, thinking that we are the intelligent ones. We can't see that we are just part of an intelligent system."[20]

This method of regenerative agriculture utilizes diverse crop cover, multiple crop rotations and managed grazing to rebuild soil nutrients resulting in increased crop yields and carbon sequestration. Each crop adds to the whole by fixing nitrogen, providing shade, crowding out weeds or repelling pests.

Recent large-scale syntropic farming of wheat, soybeans and corn has shown positive outcomes for grain production.[21]

Cuba adopted organic agricultural practices in the early 1990s after the overthrow of the Soviet Union brought shortages of conventional fertilizers and pesticides. I recently toured an organic farm in the Viñales region of Cuba where marigolds, basil and other fragrant plants are used as pest control interspersed in crop rows. Tobacco leaf stems discarded in the cigar-making process are fermented and used as fertilizer along with excrement from rabbits raised on the farm.

Organic farm, Finca Agroecológica
El Paraiso, Viñales, Cuba

Medicinal plants serve a dual purpose of crop diversification and use by the farm workers for their health benefits.

While organic methods are better for the health of people and the environment, they still require annual inputs of organic fertilizer, which agroforestry systems do not.[22]

Agroforestry methods allow livestock to roam the forest and forage for food, distributing their excrement as they roam, fertilizing the soil. These types of pastures sequester five to ten times as much carbon in soil and above-ground biomass as conventional pastureland. Studies show that silvopasture forage is easier for ruminants to digest — lowering methane emissions — while supporting biodiversity, increasing livestock yields and protecting livestock from erratic weather. In a socialist system where livestock would be communally cared for, forested lands could maintain biodiversity and at the same time provide food for livestock, rather than destroying entire ecosystems to clear grazing land.

Managed grazing, where herds are moved frequently from one grazing area to another, also greatly reduces methane production and adds nutrients to the soil. In contrast, large-scale farms collect animal waste in large lagoons and livestock are fed diets that are more difficult to digest than grasses — and both cause elevated methane emissions, which are greatly reduced through traditional practices.

Regenerative practices increase carbon capture, reduce emissions, increase yields and protect and improve soil nutrients for the long term, and are more adaptable to climate impacts due to the diversity of plants that build a more resilient ecosystem.[23]

Under capitalism, despite proof of the long-term benefits to human health and the global climate, these holistic regenerative methods are viewed as impractical and an obstacle to profits. ☐

Chapter 3

The role of the oceans

SHIFTING to a post-carbon economy is crucial for the restoration of the marine ecosystem as a carbon capture and oxygen-producing mechanism for the planet.

Oceans are the world's largest carbon sink, sequestering more carbon dioxide than all the forests combined. The microscopic phytoplankton, crucial to life on Earth, serve the same function as trees by absorbing carbon dioxide and emitting oxygen. For every ten breaths we take, seven can be attributed to this aquatic life-support system[1] that has absorbed a third of the carbon dioxide emitted since the Industrial Revolution.[2]

But there are limits to what the oceans can hold. The oversaturation of carbon dioxide is causing acidification triggering deficiencies in exoskeleton formation in species of coral, sea urchins and mollusks to the detriment of the entire marine food chain.

For anyone who has had the opportunity to experience coral reefs firsthand, it is a window into the beauty and wonder of evolution like no other. Coral reefs are by far the most diverse marine ecosystems — one quarter of all marine species rely on reefs for food or shelter. Healthy reefs not only produce oxygen, but provide a staple protein for island and coastal communities and protect coastlines from the effects of storms and sea level rise. A U.N. report from the Food and Agriculture Organization states that 17 percent of globally-consumed animal protein comes from reef fish, with that number increasing to 70 percent for island nations.[3][4]

The warming climate is threatening this crucial habitat. An article entitled, "Improved Estimates of Ocean Heat Content from 1960 to 2015," shows that our planet has already lost half of its coral and that oceanic warming is occurring 13 percent faster[5] than previ-

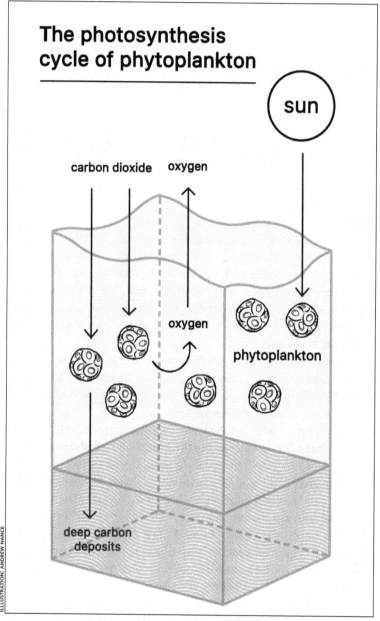

*Like terrestrial-based plants, phytoplankton use
photosynthesis to turn sunlight into chemical energy,
consuming carbon dioxide and releasing oxygen.*

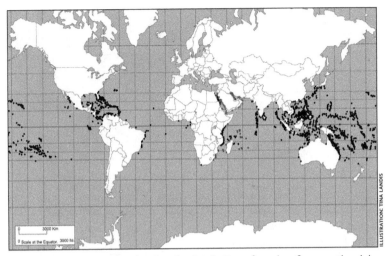

Map showing the distribution of coral reefs across the globe

ously believed — and that rate is accelerating. If we continue with "business as usual," all coral reefs are expected to be lost by 2050 due to warmer water temperatures, acidification, shipping, overfishing, coastal development and agricultural run-off.[6]

The Great Barrier Reef, the largest in the world at 133,000 square miles, has experienced four major bleaching events since 1998, with two consecutive events in 2016 and 2017. Bleaching occurs when water temperatures rise and remain elevated. Coral have a symbiotic relationship with microscopic algae. The process of photosynthesis in algae that live inside the coral provide the coral with energy and food. When temperatures rise, the algae release a toxin, and as a survival mechanism, the coral expel the algae. If temperatures remain elevated, the coral does not take the algae back in, and the coral dies.[7]

Disruption of a stable climate is also bringing bleaching events due to unusually cold waters, like in the Florida Keys in 2010 when water temperatures dropped more than 12 F below normal levels.[8]

WHAT CAN WE DO TO HELP THE OCEANS?

Research projects around the globe are showing great potential to help reefs adapt to changing ocean temperatures, but lack of funding and international cooperation stand in the way of comprehensive implementation.

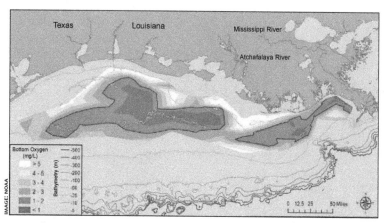

Annually-occurring dead zone
at the mouth of the Mississippi River

Researchers with the Australian Institute of Marine Science are working to find super corals that have survived bleaching events that can then be grown in labs and returned to the reef to proliferate, essentially accelerating evolution to match the fast changing climate.[9]

Another promising research project out of the University of Miami focuses on a heat-resistant algal species, *Symbiodinium clade D*, that can repopulate the coral despite sustained elevated water temperatures. Tests have been successful in lab settings, but have yet to be tested in the open ocean.[10]

Long-term systemic changes that affect ocean health can relieve additional stressors on the reefs and slow the warming of the oceans.

Industrial agriculture and lawn care rely on annual use of nitrogen-rich fertilizers, rather than using regenerative methods where the plants themselves enrich soil nutrients. Run-off from these chemically fertilized lands causes algae blooms due to the high nutrient ratio in the water. As the algae dies and decomposes, the process depletes the water of oxygen, killing off any marine life in the area, causing dead zones. One of the largest dead zones occurs annually in the Gulf of Mexico at the Mississippi River Delta.[11]

Shifting away from chemical-dependent agriculture to regenerative practices can help eliminate these massive die-offs of marine life and risks to human health from the neurotoxins produced by the algae blooms.

Another threat to reef habitats is the increasing frequency and strength of hurricanes and typhoons. On a recent trip to Guanahaca-bibes Peninsula National Park in Cuba, I witnessed their restoration program that gathers broken staghorn coral after storms and regrows them in underwater nurseries and, once mature, replants them on the reef. Keeping a strong reef system protects the Cuban coastline from taking the brunt of ever-increasing storms. As sea levels rise and reefs are at greater depths, human intervention in maintaining the protective function of barrier reefs is crucial.

The Cuban program also tracks sea turtle populations which nest on several coastal areas throughout the island. Sea turtles play a crucial role in maintaining oxygen-producing seagrass beds and add nutrients to coastal sand dunes where they nest, encouraging plant growth.[12]

Marine scientists are seeing the negative effects of rising surface temperatures on the sex determination of sea turtle hatchlings, which occurs after the eggs are laid. As temperatures increase and stay elevated, more eggs are developing as female, causing challenges to procreation in future generations. Using natural solutions, such as foliage for intermittent shade on the nests, can help regulate the temperatures and balance the sex determination.

To protect and restore the ocean systems in a comprehensive way, what is needed is the decarbonization of our economy to insure that temperatures will not increase more than 1.5 C above preindustrial levels and to minimize ocean acidification.

Most of the warming and acidification in the oceans occur in the surface waters and is causing a rapid decline in the food chain at a rate of 4 to 8 percent annually — far faster than models predicted. What makes oceans productive are upwellings of nutrient-rich cold waters from the ocean depths. As surface waters warm these natural mechanisms of overturning circulation are slowing — causing lifeless ocean "deserts" to expand.

Like the restoration of depleted land through agroforestry outlined in the previous chapter, marine permaculture can restore ocean deserts and fish productivity by reactivating the biological pump of the oceans.

Research by Dr. Brian von Herzen demonstrates the use of lightweight structures submerged just below the surface that serve as an anchor for kilometer-scale kelp forests. As these structures rise and fall with wave action, they bring nutrient-rich waters from below,

PHOTO: MIMI HAYAKAWA

*Coral nursery, Guanahacabibes
Peninsula National Park, Cuba*

attracting an abundance of life to otherwise lifeless waters. More life means more oxygen and a cooler atmosphere with the added benefit of serving as a food source for local communities.

Kelp is the fastest growing tree on earth, growing up to two feet per day. This rapidly renewing plant can be harvested and used for biofuel and bioplastics, at the same time restoring the ecosystem without the detrimental effect of other sources like palm oil and corn that destroy ecosystems and divert vital food crops.[13] [14]

THE PROBLEM OF PLASTICS

Plastics in our oceans are becoming a threat to all forms of life — aquatic and terrestrial. Microplastics are in the seafood that we eat, in the stomachs of whales, in the sea salt on our tables, in the air we breathe and even in the snow in the remote Arctic Circle.[15]

While plastic has served a useful purpose, in most cases it can be replaced with reusable or biodegradable materials. Ninety percent of current plastics could be made from rapidly renewing plants such as kelp. If we continue at the current annual rate of plastic production, at 83 pounds of plastic per person, plastics will outweigh fish in the oceans by 2050.[16]

Marine permaculture has the potential to restore life in ocean deserts by bringing nutrient-rich waters from the depths.

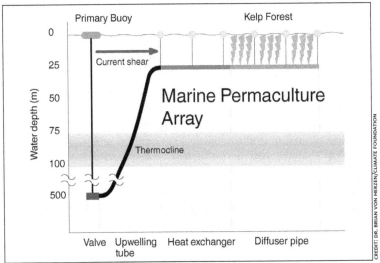

CREDIT: DR. BRIAN VON HERZEN/CLIMATE FOUNDATION

The Ocean Cleanup has already recovered plastics from the ocean and aims to develop sustainable products from it.

A study out of the Ghent University in Belgium calculated that those who regularly consume shellfish are also ingesting some 11,000 particles of plastic in their seafood annually.[17]

We must greatly reduce throw-away items and packaging. As ecologist Barry Commoner outlined in his four laws of ecology, "Everything must go somewhere." In other words, there is no "away" to throw your trash.[18]

Trash that ends up in the ocean accumulates in five subtropical ocean currents or gyres around the world — the largest, called the Great Pacific Garbage Patch, sits between Hawaii and California. Massive reduction in throw-away items, replacement of plastic with bioplastics, and extensive clean-up efforts are needed to heal the marine ecosystem.

The Ocean Cleanup project has designed a passive floatation system that works with wind and wave action and is able to remove plastics from millimeters in size to large debris such as "ghost nets." At full deployment the systems could capture 90 percent of ocean plastics by 2040, and in the process, pose no harm to sea life or shipping vessels.[19]

SEAFOOD: THE CASH CROP OF THE OCEANS

Under capitalism, everything that brings high profits is like a gold rush until the source dries up — and seafood is the ocean's cash crop.

Industrial-scale overfishing contributes major stressors to the marine ecosystem. When key species are wiped out or greatly diminished, a domino effect occurs within the entire food chain, weakening all functions of the ecosystem.

Annual catches have been decreasing by nearly one million tons annually since the 1990s, due to species depletion. Through the incredibly wasteful industrial trawling process, millions of tons of bycatch are caught annually and discarded. Industrial trawling practices also release large quantities of carbon dioxide into the atmosphere by disturbing the captured carbon embedded in the sea floor.

Eliminating industrial fishing practices and shifting to locally-run sustainable fisheries can strengthen ocean ecosystems by avoiding overfishing of any one species. Sustainable fishing cooperatives run by coastal communities — who have the greatest knowledge of their local ecosystem — operate with the long-term health of the oceans in mind.[20]

A shift to sustainable fishing along with ocean clean up, marine permaculture and a shift to regenerative agriculture to prevent dead zones from run-off are all needed to maintain the oceans as an oxygen-producing system to sustain life above and below the seas. □

Chapter 4

Our warming world

THE ocean currents play a major role in what happens in the atmosphere. As ice melts and water heats up, the major ocean currents around the globe are shifting, which sets in motion changes in weather patterns that are causing unprecedented droughts, floods, and more frequent and extreme temperature anomalies and storms.

Mild climates like northern Europe are seeing record heat waves and droughts,[1] while equatorial islands like Palau have shifted from two distinct wet and dry seasons to rain all year long.[2]

As temperature ranges shift, vector-borne diseases such as malaria and dengue may spread to northern regions. Malaria currently kills 1 million people annually, mostly children.[3]

The Arctic Circle is warming nearly twice as fast as other regions causing shifting patterns in the jet stream and extreme weather events, like the polar vortex that brought wind chills of -65 F to the Midwest region of the United States in early 2019 and trapped warmer air to the north.[4] Remote communities in the Arctic that have historically used frozen waters as transport routes and access to hunting grounds are now facing challenges to their survival due to melting ice.[5]

In May 2019, temperatures reached 84 F in Russia near the entrance to the Arctic Ocean at the same time that atmospheric concentrations of carbon dioxide reached 415 ppm, the highest ever recorded in human history. Carbon dioxide remains in the atmosphere for 100 to 150 years, meaning we are only now feeling the combined warming effects of carbon dioxide that was released more than a century ago through today.[6] Recent studies suggest that carbon can in fact remain in the atmosphere thousands of years longer once the natural absorption capacity of the planet's land and water is reached.[7]

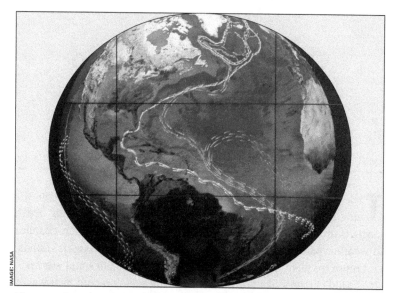

IMAGE: NASA

There are signs that the weakening of the Atlantic circulation has an effect on U.S. fisheries and storms. Ice melting off Greenland as the Arctic warms is believed to play a key role.

FEEDBACK LOOPS

Ice reflects the heat of the sun acting as a giant air conditioning mechanism for the atmosphere. As the massive ice sheets at the poles melt and expose less reflective water and land, heat is absorbed rather than reflected, causing further heating of the atmosphere and more ice loss, perpetuating a warming spiral. Additionally, as ice sheets on Antarctica and Greenland melt, freshwater that was trapped on land in the form of ice flows into the ocean and raises sea levels.

The potential rapid release of methane from permafrost is another volatile feedback loop that most climate models do not take into account. Researchers are particularly concerned about a massive shelf of underwater permafrost in the East Siberian Sea, which has reached 0 C, while its land-based equivalent is still much cooler at -10 C.[8]

As warmer water currents continue to flow into the shallow seas of the Arctic, sea floor permafrost begins to melt, releasing the methane that has been trapped for hundreds of thousands of years. Scientists have recently discovered a "hot spot" of approximately one thousand square kilometers with 60 million methane bubble

THE CHANGING JET STREAM

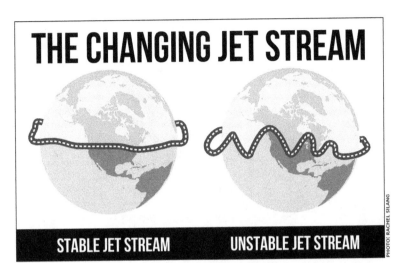

STABLE JET STREAM   UNSTABLE JET STREAM

PHOTO: RACHEL SILANG

*Climate change is creating an unstable jet stream,
pushing higher temperatures northward and
bringing sub-zero temperatures to the south.*

plumes,[9] far exceeding the normal rate of around tens of thousands for that area. This potent greenhouse gas, if released from the melting seabed, could push us past a tipping point.[10]

RISING WATERS

The effects of rising seas that we are currently experiencing are mainly due to the expansion of warming water and melting of the Greenland ice sheet. We have yet to feel the effect of major melting of land-based ice sheets in Antarctica, which alone could raise sea levels by 60 meters.[11]

Reports from the U.N. Intergovernmental Panel on Climate Change are far more conservative than many independent scientists' estimates of sea level rise and do not take into account the melting Antarctica and Greenland ice sheets. Dr. Harold Wanless of the University of Miami stated that a "ten-foot rise by 2050 is very plausible."[12]

Low-lying coastal regions like the Miami area are already experiencing "sunny day flooding" on a regular basis when high tides bring sea water into the streets. When king tides and storm surges occur, flooding becomes more widespread. In areas such as this, sea walls cannot keep the rising waters at bay. Sitting on porous limestone,

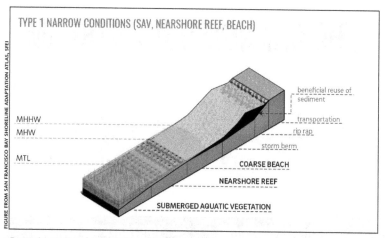

Restoring natural wetlands and reef systems
can absorb rising seas and protect coastal areas.

the sea water seeps up from below creating "springs" throughout the coastal region as sea level rises. This also causes salinization of agricultural land and septic systems to become inundated and back up into homes.

With 400 miles of densely populated shoreline, much of the San Francisco Bay Area is equally vulnerable. Yet, developers are continuing to build on low-lying land, like Mission Bay and Bayview-Hunters Point in San Francisco, despite sea level rise models showing that these areas will be underwater with just a five-foot increase.[13]

Recently a group of ecosystem scientists and urban planners joined forces to draft the San Francisco Bay Shoreline Adaptation Atlas[14] that utilizes natural solutions including a ring of man-made reefs, graded marshlands and rocky beaches surrounding the estuary. Rather than building sea walls to repel rising waters, their solutions work with the ecosystem and wildlife to absorb the rising tides. Lead author of the study Julie Beagle stressed that the projects need to begin within the next few years for the natural environments to mature to a level effective for coastal protection before the changes occur.[15]

We must face the reality of sea level rise, and where necessary, begin to relocate vulnerable communities to higher ground and address industrial facilities at risk of flooding. The Nuclear Regulatory Commission refuses to even acknowledge the looming catastrophe in relation to coastal nuclear power plants that risk inundation and critical breeches of radioactive material as waters rise and storms become more violent. The 2011 reactor meltdown at the Fukushima Daiichi nuclear plant in Japan caused by an earthquake-triggered tsunami should inspire immediate action.[16]

A people/planet-centered government would already be preparing for inundation by shutting down coastal nuclear sites, cleaning up polluted land and removing toxins from buildings that will damage the marine ecosystem when flooding occurs — which it will. For a preview of the coming crisis, we can look to the lack of government preparedness prior to Hurricane Harvey in the Gulf Coast and tropical storm Florence that hit North Carolina, both of which led to the release of massive amounts of toxic pollutants into the environment from the inundation of industrial and large-scale agricultural facilities.

Instead of action, city governments and developers in low-lying regions are downplaying the crisis in order to maintain their tax base and keep profits rolling in — another example of how capitalism is hamstringing adaptation to the coming changes.

At the same time as we hear endless excuses about why there are no funds for infrastructure and services that benefit the people, tax breaks for corporations and the super-rich occur annually. Sixty Fortune 500 companies paid no federal taxes in 2018, and two — Chevron and Netflix, headquartered in the San Francisco Bay Area — got $200 million each in tax rebates.[17] Comprehensive infrastructure projects to protect populations and the environment are rarely implemented under capitalism — and never in an efficient timeframe — because they are not profitable.

THE COMING FIRESTORM

Historically, wildfires have been part of the natural cycle of a healthy forest adding soil nutrients, creating space for light to reach the forest floor, and eliminating pests and disease. Today, the severity and frequency of wildfires, combined with increased climate stressors, results in forests struggling to recover and firestorms incinerating entire towns.[18]

The warming world is witnessing an increase in wildfires that are occurring in areas that rarely saw fires in the past. In the summer of 2019, wildfires raged above the Arctic Circle throughout Greenland,

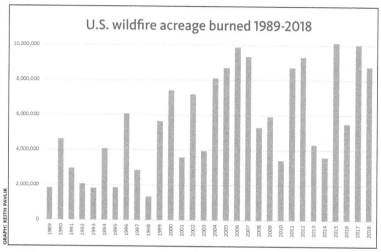

Wildfires have spiked dramatically in the in the last two decades.

Russia, Canada and Alaska.[19] Longer periods of hot, dry weather have increased wildfire season in the western United States from seven months to all year long.[20]

California saw the two most destructive wildfires in its history with the 2017 Tubbs Fire and 2018 Camp Fire that destroyed the entire town of Paradise. Both were started by sparks from power lines run by the private statewide utility Pacific Gas and Electric. Compensation and liability claims will be tied up in the courts for years, with PG&E making a token gesture of putting the new lines it is installing in Paradise underground to protect against future liability.

In a people/planet-centered society, the utility would be under public control, all power lines would be underground and housing would be relocated away from fire-prone areas. But instead under capitalism, the rights of the corporation come first and any compensation PG&E is forced to pay will be squeezed out of their customers through rate increases with no change in land use policy that would impede developers' profits.

In addition to the relocation of populations from high-risk areas, restoring the health of forests through reforestation methods outlined in the previous chapter can help build forest resilience, lower temperatures and retain more soil moisture, all of which can aid prevention and recovery.

While we need implementation of comprehensive preparedness measures, we must also immediately cut global greenhouse
gas emissions to minimize the warming of the planet. There is no
time for market-based solutions or incremental changes that protect
corporate profits.

RENEWABLES CAN MEET
WORLDWIDE ENERGY NEEDS TODAY

I first became optimistic about climate solutions when I heard
Stanford professor and environmental engineer Mark Jacobson present
his report showing evidence that all global energy needs could be
powered by wind, water and solar (WWS) today. In an attempt to
debunk the report, individuals tied to the nuclear and carbon capture
industries, along with the National Academy of Sciences, subsequently
published a critique claiming there were modeling flaws.[21] Jacobson's
follow-up 2018 report dispelled these critiques and demonstrated capacity to achieve total WWS power generation in 139 countries by 2050.[22]

The entire United States could be powered on wind energy from
the wind capacity of just three states — Kansas, North Dakota and
Texas.[23] Despite the great potential, wind power globally sees a fraction
in energy subsidies of what fossil fuels receive — $12.3 billion over 17
years for wind compared to $5.3 trillion given to the fossil fuel industry
in 2015 alone![24]

Wind power uses 98 to 99 percent less water resources than fossil
fuel power generation,[25] while coal, gas and nuclear suck up a combined total of 22 to 62 trillion gallons per year.[26] Currently, 3.7 percent
of global energy comes from wind and that number is increasing. Wind
powers 10 million homes in Spain, 40 percent of Denmark's energy
needs, 15 percent of Uruguay's, and China installed 31 gigawatts of new
capacity in 2015 alone.[27]

Interconnected grids, and distributed production and energy
storage, serve to alleviate the challenges of the intermittent supply of
wind and solar.

Microgrids are local groupings of distributed energy sources like
wind and solar that encompass production, storage and load management systems. They can function as stand-alone systems — particularly
well suited for rural areas in Africa and Asia — or can function within
a larger grid. Microgrids demonstrate higher efficiency due to localized

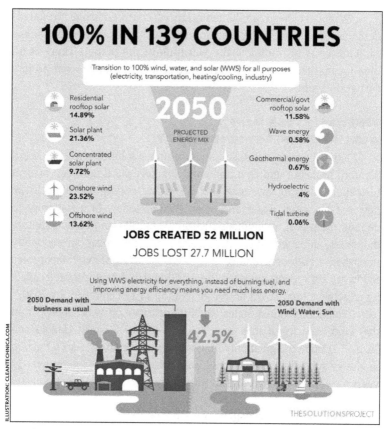

Wind, water and solar energy can meet the world's energy needs today.

production and consumption that eliminates energy loss through long distance delivery and are more resilient in meeting local demands. In the industrialized world, energy monopolies stand in the way of microgrid adoption, whereas in the developing world where no grid currently exists, microgrids and stand-alone solar are a practical zero-emission solution to electrification.

Solar and micro-wind are allowing communities that have never had electricity to leapfrog over fossil fuels directly to renewables. By 2014, three million solar home systems had been installed in off-grid rural communities in Bangladesh as part of the government's goal to reach universal electricity access by 2021.[28]

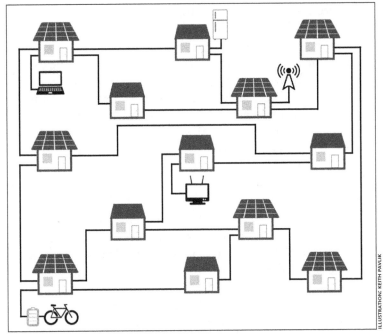

*Microgrids can connect multiple energy producers
and users to share energy and balance load.*

Geothermal, wave and tidal energy production are largely untapped resources due to lack of investment, but have great potential to add to the renewable grid.

The nuclear, fossil fuel and carbon capture lobbyists continue to block progress on renewable adoption claiming that it is impossible to transition without grid failure and frequent blackouts.

NUCLEAR POWER: A FALSE SOLUTION

While being touted as a low-carbon form of energy, nuclear is lumped in with renewable sources ignoring life-cycle carbon emissions, as well as the insurmountable problem of reactor waste and the risk of catastrophic accidents. Lifecycle emissions of nuclear are third highest after scrubbed coal-fired plants and natural gas.[29]

In Ohio, legislation is being considered to create a so-called Clean Air Fund that would solely benefit nuclear and exclude funding for wind and solar.[30]

Reactors are incredibly costly to build and maintain, but due to a powerful lobby, new reactor construction and operation get massive government subsidies. Treating nuclear as a renewable energy source equal to wind, water and solar discounts true sustainable energy production.

The World Nuclear Association is promoting the construction of 1,000 new reactors by 2050 — that is one new reactor every 12 days! — as a way to curb worldwide carbon dioxide emissions. If implemented, their $8.2 trillion scheme would only offset less than 10 percent of the carbon dioxide reductions needed.[31]

As long as the system is driven by profits — with lobbyists buying politicians and the courts protecting the rights of corporations — we will never see a livable future. False solutions promoted by nuclear, fossil fuel and carbon-capture industries are merely a costly distraction that reaps profits for a few in the short term while wasting precious time that could be spent on comprehensible renewable adoption.

ENERGY DEVELOPMENT IN THE GLOBAL SOUTH

I often hear criticism from the left about fossil fuel and nuclear energy development in countries of the Global South, such as Iran's reliance on nuclear energy, China's use of coal-fired power plants or the socialist government of Venezuela's use of oil profits to fund its extensive social benefits programs. In the global, eco-socialist future, these countries will not need to rely on unsustainable energy sources. But in the present day, we must assess each nation's sustainable development within the context of world imperialism and how the Global North can support a just transition for these nations instead of contributing to the problem of colonial and neo-colonial domination.

The legacy of underdevelopment imposed on the Global South by the northern colonizers has left these countries decades behind in energy and infrastructure development. The ongoing hostility towards these nations keeps them under the boot of imperialism and blocks sustainable development. Under the imperialist capitalist world order, nations that choose an independent path in the development of nuclear energy must live with constant threat and harassment from the United States and their European partners, as we see with Iran. The imperialists feign concern for the safety and security of the

U.S. SANCTIONED COUNTRIES

U.S. sanctions limit access to technology and resources, hindering sustainable development.

people as the reason for these restrictions, but in truth it is about retaining global dominance.

In the eco-socialist future, international relations will be based on cooperation rather than domination and competition, which continue to hinder developmental progress in the Global South. Under socialism, it will be the duty of wealthier nations to assist other countries to achieve zero-carbon energy systems in return for their centuries of plunder.

These same principles will be applied with respect for the sovereignty of Native nations and the self-determination of communities which have been disproportionately impacted by climate change and environmental injustice. Addressing the global climate requires a new society that shares technology and resources free of imperialist domination and the legacy of racism. Only then can all nations attain renewable energy production and solve our shared crisis. ☐

Chapter 5

The ecological footprint of capitalism

HE very nature of the capitalist system runs counter to sustainability. Under capitalism, corporations must constantly find new markets, produce more and increase profits within the expand-or-die system. What is needed is centralized planning to produce only what is needed for society using the most sustainable, low-carbon methods possible.

In their book entitled "What Every Environmentalist Needs to Know About Capitalism," John Bellamy Foster and Fred Magdoff highlight the impossibility of "green" capitalism explaining that capitalism is "a system that has only one goal, the maximization of profits in an endless quest for the accumulation of capital on an ever-expanding scale, and which thus seeks to transform everything on earth into a commodity with a price, is a system that is soulless; it can never be green. It can never stand still, but is driven to manipulate and fabricate whims and wants in order to grow and sell more ... forever. Nothing is allowed to stand in its path."

They go on to explain renowned climatologist James Hansen's perspective on cap-and-trade policies as the "'temple of doom' and 'worse than nothing' because it prevents effective action directly limiting carbon through regulations and a properly designed tax, while giving people the impression that something is being done."

From the first Earth Summit held in Rio de Janeiro in 1992 through the U.N. climate summits of today, there have been no binding agreements and no significant emissions reductions. The voluntary commitments that came from the much-touted 2016 Paris Agreement have us on track to exceed 3 C, far beyond the 1.5 C increase that much of the scientific community urges as the threshold to avoid catastrophe. While some well-meaning people attend, in the end the decisions of these summits really only serve as greenwashing

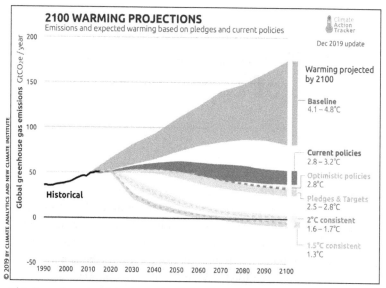

2100 WARMING PROJECTIONS
Emissions and expected warming based on pledges and current policies

Climate Action Tracker

Dec 2019 update

Warming projected by 2100

Baseline
4.1 – 4.8°C

Current policies
2.8 – 3.2°C

Optimistic policies
2.8°C

Pledges & Targets
2.5 – 2.8°C

2°C consistent
1.6 – 1.7°C

1.5°C consistent
1.3°C

Historical

Global greenhouse gas emissions GtCO₂e / year

© 2019 BY CLIMATE ANALYTICS AND NEW CLIMATE INSTITUTE

This December 2019 data shows the pledges from the much-touted Paris Agreement to limit the rise in global warming. They put the world well above the 1.5 C threshold to avoid catastrophic change.

public relations campaigns for world leaders and corporations to keep up the illusion that they are listening to science and taking action. Important interventions have been made at the summits themselves by legions of protesters, and by representatives of countries of the Global South who point out the hypocrisy of the imperialist countries in creating the problem and offloading its most direct consequences.

Notably, at the 2009 Copenhagen meeting, the Obama administration attempted to blackmail countries not to support the proposal from Bolivia and Venezuela to create binding targets on carbon emission reductions. Behind the scenes it told countries they would not receive climate adaptation aid if they did not vote for the U.S. version of the accord. A few months later, Bolivian President Evo Morales convened the World People's Conference on Climate Change and the Rights of Mother Earth in Cochabamba, attended by 15,000 delegates — which denounced the inadequacy of Copenhagen and announced clear binding targets to limit global warming to 1 C. The U.S. government and other imperialist countries boycotted the event. A decade later, they helped overthrow Morales in a military coup.

ENDLESS GROWTH MEANS ENDLESS WASTE

Post-World War II saw the birth of marketing and the consumerist culture we see today. After the war, the United States had an edge over its European counterparts, who had sustained massive destruction to their infrastructure and productive capacity. The United Sates, left largely unscathed, provided loans for Europe to rebuild and began pushing a consumer culture at home to boost the U.S. economy and compensate for the loans. This saw the rise of Madison Avenue advertising agencies and a flood of consumer products into the market.

Planned obsolescence — creating things that are made to break or wear out after a short period of time rather than made to last — and perceived obsolescence — the marketing tool that dupes consumers into buying the latest styles and products as a form of personal gratification and belonging even when last season's items are still in good condition — can only occur under the absurd system of capitalism where profits are the supreme goal.

Ninety-nine percent of products bought today are discarded within six months. Waste created from the production process alone is 70 times greater than the waste created by disposing of the products themselves.[1]

Not only is 35 to 50 percent of food wasted in the United States, but it is common business practice for restaurants and groceries to lock dumpsters so food-insecure people cannot access the discarded food because this devalues their products. A similar practice is used by the clothing industry — the second most polluting industry in the world — by cutting up last season's unsold clothing so it will not show up on the backs of the poor.

We cannot solve the crisis by simply recycling and driving electric vehicles. Cutting production and consumption levels is key. Recycling, while diverting some materials away from landfills, is a short-sighted solution to the waste problem. Producing and recycling single-use items uses valuable energy resources, most of which are currently derived from fossil fuels or nuclear. Most wealthy nations outsource the recycling process to the Global South, which adds shipping emissions. China and other countries recently stopped accepting waste from abroad, forcing some U.S. municipalities to resort to incineration of recyclable goods due to lack of local processing facilities.[2]

The real solution is to greatly reduce unnecessary production and waste, make things to last, eliminate throwaway items and packaging,

Food waste in the United States

40%
of all food produced in the U.S. is wasted

$1 billion
spent annually to dispose of food waste

$165 billion
estimated retail value of lost food

49 million people
in the U.S. are food insecure

11 million children
are food insecure

58 billion meals
could be served annually with wasted food

20%
of all landfill is food waste
more than paper or plastic

Landfills account for 34%
of all methane emissions in the U.S.

Methane has 21 times
the global warming potential of CO_2

Greenhouse gas emissions from lost or wasted food is equivalent to 37 million cars

GRAPHIC: KEITH PAVLIK

and utilize cradle-to-cradle methods in all production of the things we need. The cradle-to-cradle model, although conceived within the framework of capitalist production, can inform production methods under a socialist economy. The idea is that all components of every product can be easily disassembled after the product's lifetime into biological nutrients that degrade and are reabsorbed into the biosphere or into technical nutrients, that are recycled endlessly for reuse.[3]

This comprehensive change in the production model can only be facilitated under a socialist planned economy. Under capitalism, where the maximization of profits is the ultimate goal, companies that attempt to implement "green" practices fail due to competition and the higher production costs of sustainable products. For instance, the sportswear company Puma put together an environmental plan to "go green" in 2011 that was never implemented when the accounting showed it would lead to the company's demise.[4]

THE PENTAGON

Although the United States' endless war policy officially began with the Sept. 11 attacks on the World Trade Center, their imperialist aims began much earlier with their first colonies acquired in the Spanish American War. The immense loss of life, destruction of entire nations and the effect on the environment are incalculable — all for the enrichment of the billionaire class under the false pretense of spreading "freedom" and "democracy." Regime change efforts, sanctions, bombing campaigns and occupations destroy local ecosystems, increase poverty and disrupt local infrastructure functions. U.S. interventionist strategies undermine progressive environmental policies of left-leaning governments, as is evident after the coup against Brazil's president Dilma Rousseff and the subsequent opening up of the Amazon Basin to extractive industries by the pro-U.S. president Bolsonaro.

International climate summits never mention the fact that the Pentagon is the biggest unregulated polluter on the planet. Nine hundred of the nearly 1,200 superfund sites in the United States are former military bases. In 2016, the U.S. Navy announced its plan to release 20,000 tons of environmental "stressors," including heavy metals and explosives into the coastal waters of the Pacific Northwest.

The toxic legacy left behind from decades of bombing other countries, the use of depleted uranium munitions, weapons testing

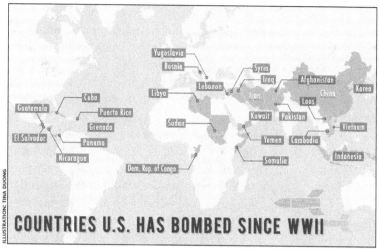

ILLUSTRATION: TINA DUONG

COUNTRIES U.S. HAS BOMBED SINCE WWII

Wars and bombing campaigns wreak environmental destruction and leave a toxic legacy for future generations.

and uranium mining for those weapons has never been quantified. The open burn pits used at U.S. bases in Iraq to dispose of waste have resulted in rampant cancer rates in U.S. soldiers and Iraqi civilians.[5] These open incinerators were used to dispose of literally everything — "petroleum, oil, rubber, tires, plastic, Styrofoam, batteries, appliances, electrical equipment, pesticides, aerosol cans, oil, explosives, casings, medical waste, and animal and human carcasses. They also used jet fuel to stoke the fire," according to The Guardian.[6]

This poisoning of the planet and humanity dates back decades from the U.S. nuclear testing on the Marshall Islands and Guam, to weapons testing in Vieques, Puerto Rico, to Agent Orange used as a defoliant in the Vietnam War, which is still causing birth defects in Vietnamese children to this day. But to the U.S. imperialist war machine, this is all just 'collateral damage' in their unending quest for control of resources and global markets at all cost.

Imperialism is the highest stage of capitalism. It is in a constant war-drive seeking new markets and resources to conquer at the expense of countless lives and the health of the planet. We must dismantle the self-perpetuating system of endless war propagated by the military-industrial complex that seeks any opportunity to foment conflict in order to sell more weapons for the immense profit of a few.

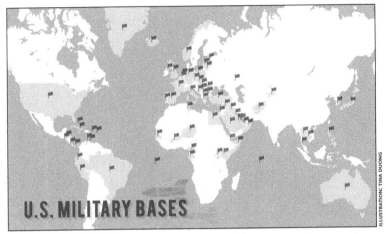

U.S. MILITARY BASES

The United States is said to have 800 military bases in more than 70 countries worldwide.

Imperialist war and militarism uphold the very system that created the climate crisis, while further contributing as a super-consumer of fossil fuels. Eliminating the military industrial complex is a crucial component for a decarbonized future.

THE ECOLOGICAL FOOTPRINT OF THE EMPIRE

The United States is the largest per capita polluter on the planet. If everyone on Earth had the ecological footprint of people in the United States, we would need five planets to sustain us. This is largely due to the obscene lifestyles of the wealthiest 1 percent, the car culture that proliferates suburban sprawl and long commutes, and all the waste and emissions that come with a consumer culture.

The Global Footprint Network calculates the Earth Overshoot Day every year. In 2018, humanity used up nature's budget (per person carbon footprint of a country versus global biocapacity per person) by Aug. 1, with the United States using up their resource allotment for the year on March 15 — meaning it used up its share of global resources in just 74 days![7]

Most carbon emission studies focus on emissions that occur within the borders of a country and do not include consumption-based carbon emissions — meaning the carbon emitted in another country in the process of making the stuff you buy. In 2016, a consump-

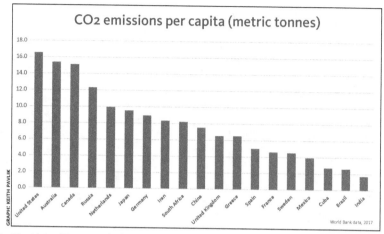

GRAPH: KEITH PAVLIK

*The United States is the largest
per capita polluter on the planet.*

tion-based greenhouse gas inventory was created for the San Francisco Bay Area and showed that emissions were in reality around 35 percent higher than the emissions produced within the Bay Area. Meaning if you take into account the access to goods in the United States that were manufactured elsewhere, the per capita carbon footprint is actually much higher when outsourcing of production is taken into account. Remember this when the United States points a finger at China for its emissions levels.[8]

This is more evidence backing the argument that the wealthy nations hold more responsibility for the problem since the vast majority of the goods produced overseas end up being purchased in the richer nations. □

Chapter 6

Transforming
how we live and work

I N an eco-socialist economy, the way we live and work will be sustainable for people and the planet.

Today, heating, cooling and lighting the places where we live, work and play accounts for 40 percent of total energy consumption. That number reflects the major inefficiencies of the aging infrastructure across the United States. The World Bank estimates 8.6 trillion gallons of water are lost each year from leaks, half of which occur in wealthier nations.[1]

Although retrofitting aging structures would greatly reduce energy consumption, under capitalism, it is up to the individual property owner to make these improvements.

Under a socialist system, a comprehensive retrofitting plan would be implemented nationwide resulting in immediate energy savings. For instance, socialist Cuba distributed pressure cookers, rice cookers and energy efficient refrigerators to households throughout the nation as part of their 2007 Energy Revolution. Cuba also became the first nation to completely eliminate inefficient incandescent bulbs through distribution of compact fluorescent bulbs to 100 percent of households.[2]

Buildings can be retrofitted or rebuilt as net zero energy structures incorporating smart windows that utilize sunlight for heating and cooling, cool roofs that mitigate the heat island effect by lowering air temperatures, heat pumps that capture and recycle energy from waste, distributed energy storage from on-site solar and microwind, and building automation to maximize efficiency.[3]

Green roofs have great potential benefits because they provide building insulation, capture rainwater and carbon, and create habitats for insects and birds, but they are currently not sustainable due to the large amounts of plastics and Styrofoam used as their base.

Key Development and Sustainability for Cuba and the United States		
	Cuba	U.S.
Life expectancy	79 years	79 years
Literacy rate	100%	99%
Infant mortality (per 1000 live births)	4	6
Percent of children with low birth rate	5.3	8.0
Percent of children enrolled in primary school	98	95
Public expenditure on education (% of GDP)	12.8	5.0
Electricity consumption per capita (kWh)	1,451	12,994
CO_2 emissions per capita	2.1	15.0
Data compiled from United Nations and World Bank, 2010-2019		

CHART: KEITH PAVLIK

Despite the crippling U.S. blockade, socialist Cuba ranks highest on the Sustainable Development Index, while the United States ranks 159.

Bioplastics and lightweight mycelium-based materials can be sustainable substitutes.[4]

Today, we see a few wealthy institutions and individuals building more sustainable structures. The changes needed cannot and should not be based on those neighborhoods, cities or individuals who can afford the investment in sustainability. We cannot tackle the crisis of climate change and long-term sustainability in a piecemeal way that would leave behind the majority of the working class. It must be solved through a planned socialist economy with a systematic implementation of the changes to benefit all in an efficient, egalitarian and impactful manner.

The very foundation of how we live, move around and access goods and services must shift to align with the needs of the people and planet rather than to facilitate the flow of capital.

The mass marketing campaign launched after WW II equating a house in the suburbs with happiness and success served to enrich developers and car companies while greatly increasing carbon emissions and creating the current commuter culture. In 1960, one-third of the U.S. population lived in suburbs, a third in rural

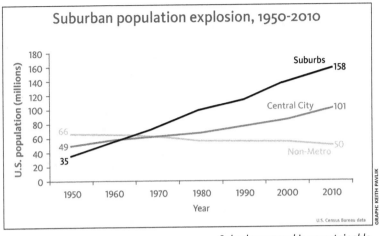

Suburban population explosion, 1950-2010

Suburban sprawl is unsustainable,
yet continues to soar in the United States.

areas, and a third in cities. By 1990, over half the population lived in the suburbs.[5]

Today, the house in the suburbs is still a mark of status for certain sectors of the population, while many are being forced out of urban centers into long daily commutes by the rising costs of urban housing. In San Francisco, the average rent for a one-bedroom apartment as of November 2019 was $3,513.[6] A Department of Housing and Urban Development report showed that an annual wage below $117,000 now qualifies as low-income in three Bay Area counties.[7] Most cities are seeing a similar trend in skyrocketing housing costs, which in turn raises transportation-related emissions as large sectors of the population are forced into longer commutes to urban job centers.

Transportation is the single largest sector contributing to greenhouse gas emissions in the United States, accounting for 29 percent of GHG emissions nationally and increasing to 41 percent in metropolitan regions like the San Francisco Bay Area.[8][9]

Just from a climate standpoint — not to mention the humanitarian crisis that results from a lack of affordable housing — unregulated housing costs are not sustainable. How can we address emissions, when large sectors of the population are forced to drive sometimes 50 to over 100 miles in their daily commutes? Even if all regions had zero-emission reliable public transit or electric vehicles, it is not a

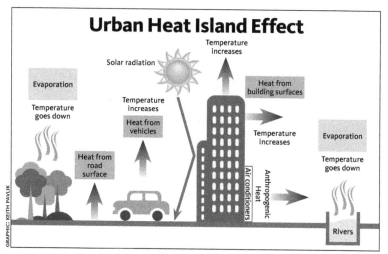

Pavement, rooftops and lack of green spaces
greatly increase air temperatures in urban areas.

sustainable use of resources to move large sectors of the population such long distances on a daily basis.

TOWARD AN ECO-SOCIALIST FUTURE

U.S. cities were designed for the automobile — and this car-centered culture has now spread globally. Wide streets; long distances between housing, services and jobs; a web of freeways connecting metropolitan centers to suburban sprawl of single-family housing tracts to shopping malls and business parks, all serve to enrich the auto and fossil fuel industries at the expense of quality of life and the climate. The majority of urban planning revolves around the car — moving and parked. In Los Angeles, parking lots and parking spaces account for 17,020,594 square meters (183,208,149 square feet) of land, equal in size to nearly 1,400 soccer fields.[10]

These vast paved areas, along with dark roof top surfaces, trap the heat of the sun, creating an urban heat island effect that increases air temperatures by as much as 44 F. Pavement, unlike a natural landscape, does not allow urban areas to cool down overnight. During prolonged heat waves, which are becoming more frequent, heat-related deaths are on the rise.[11] Converting just five percent of pavement and roofs to "cool" versions could lower urban temperatures by 1.8 F.[12]

In the eco-socialist future, cities will be integrated into the ecosystem.

In the sustainable future, cities will be restructured to provide jobs, education, health care, cultural and recreation centers within walking and biking distance to housing, and all areas easily accessible to those with mobility challenges. Cities will be integrated into the ecosystem for the enjoyment of all residents and will include urban gardens and natural areas that capture carbon, lower air temperatures and add soil moisture.[13]

The urban-rural divide will be overcome with equal access to housing, jobs, education, healthcare and culture in rural areas. Remote communities will be linked through high-speed rail, and where needed, zero-emission communally-owned vehicles.

An integral feature of suburban housing development in the United States is the lawn, making it the single largest irrigated "crop" and a highly profitable $51 billion industry.[14] Converting 49,000 square miles of land into a strictly controlled monocrop ecosystem of lawns requires large quantities of water and chemical fertilizers to maintain. Run-off from these lawns is a major contributor to the algal blooms that cause ocean dead zones as has been previously discussed.[15]

In an ecologically sustainable society, gardens of native plant species adapted to the local climate will replace lawns, contributing to soil nutrients and moisture. Instead of every household maintaining a lawn, centrally-located sustainable lawn areas appropriate for sports and recreation will be shared by the community.

Those who currently live in housing that exceeds their needs will live in smaller housing units. Dense housing areas will be supplemented by shared spaces for recreation, relaxation and socializing. Communal free child care centers will provide learning and recreation for children, which will support parents in child-rearing.

All the household drudgery that takes up our limited free time — especially that of women and caregivers — will be available to all through the socialist system in the form of communal laundries, and cleaning and maintenance services will be based on local needs. Communal kitchens serving healthy, organic and locally-sourced food for all dietary needs will be provided in each neighborhood block. These services would save not only individuals' time but also would reduce the carbon footprint of each household by consolidating energy and water usage needed for cooking and washing into fewer locations.

While certain workers may have natural inclinations and skills in a certain type of labor, the idea of a lifelong career would be the exception. Workers would have opportunities to regularly get retrained in new fields and skills so that no one would be stuck in the same job for long periods of time, but would be encouraged to be lifelong learners and contribute in various ways throughout their lives to benefit society. Service tasks that need less training, like laundry and kitchen duty, cleaning services and gardening, would be shared on a rotating basis by all those able to work. And we would all work less with more time for study, recreation and cultural activities.

These solutions show a positive egalitarian way forward. By reducing our individual footprint and collectivizing labor to meet society's needs, we can lessen the individual burden and our overall ecological footprint.

Some may say this is utopian, that humans are naturally greedy and will take advantage of the system and not do their fair share. If we divide up the existence of humanity into 365 days, only the last few days have occurred under a class-structured society. For most of our existence, we lived in communal societies where work and resources were shared by all.

Under capitalism, we are forced to compete with each other for a job, school admission and housing. The system brings out the worst in humans and degrades our interactions to those of competition rather than cooperation. Our daily interactions are most often tied to monetary exchanges for goods and services and it is a rare case of generosity when someone gives their time or resources for free. When natural disasters occur, like hurricanes Harvey or Katrina in the Gulf Coast region, we get glimpses of our potential through the personal sacrifice and heroism of strangers helping each other. But there is another way forward where this behavior becomes the norm rather than the exception. The eco-socialist transformation will be an evolutionary step forward and an embrace of our communal past resulting in a society based on cooperation that will foster the best qualities of humanity while protecting the ecosystem. ☐

Chapter 7

The economics
of transformation

WHEN government officials and political pundits proclaim that even moderate legislative proposals such as the Green New Deal are utopian, they do so because of their allegiance to the system of capitalism, not because the plan itself is unattainable for humanity. Under the current capitalist system, fossil fuels are intricately tied to all aspects of the economy and trade. Fossil fuels are currently used to create nearly everything in our society — from the power used to harvest food and light and heat buildings; to transportation; to being imbedded in many of the products we use. The managers of the U.S. capitalist system will always resist decarbonizing our economy because the value of the dollar is married to the value of oil.

It is not about getting a few more progressives in Congress or pushing them to make change. We literally cannot move forward to a post-carbon world without a shift to a socialist system because of the inextricable link between oil and the dollar and the capitalist law of profit.

Under capitalism, the world's poor always suffer the most — from lack of access to healthy food and economic opportunities, to toxic pollution in our neighborhoods, to lack of green spaces proven to greatly benefit overall well-being, to mass displacement due to conflict and climate change. Due to lack of financial means and political power, poor communities — especially poor communities of color — are disregarded in the quest for profits; that is, until we organize and fight back. But any gains by the people are piecemeal and temporary under capitalism. A community may win against one toxic polluter, but then another moves in down the road. Our water, soil, food and homes are poisoned with pesticides, herbicides, pharmaceuticals and

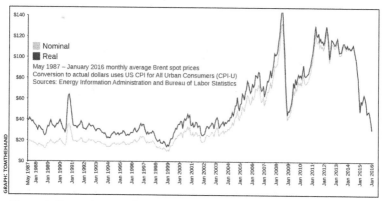

The capitalist market is so dependent on oil
that the boom and bust cycles of crude and
the dollar are inextricably linked.

more than 80,000 manufactured chemicals — 20,000 of which are
protected as "trade secrets" with unknown composition or harms.[1]

Climate change is already having catastrophic impacts on poor
communities around the globe and displacing millions worldwide.
The rich think they can escape — and in the short term they can —
because they have the financial means to pay for increasingly scarce
drinking water and healthy food, the ability to simply relocate to
another one of their many properties when one of their homes is
destroyed by flood or wildfire. The cynical get-rich-quick scheme of
disaster capitalism has the billionaires salivating at each new conflict
and environmental catastrophe. Private security and reconstruction
contractors, along with skyrocketing home insurance premiums are
increasing the wealth of the ruling class while the world burns and
the majority suffers.

This sick cycle can and must be overturned.

The very purpose of the U.S. government is to protect the interests of the ruling class. The courts act in favor of corporations' rights
over those of society. When an environmental regulation is proposed,
the regulation must be "economically feasible" for corporations to
implement — meaning environmental protections only occur when
they align with profits or when there is a mass sustained people's
movement demanding them, and only insofar as the movement's
activities do not impede the profit-making apparatus.

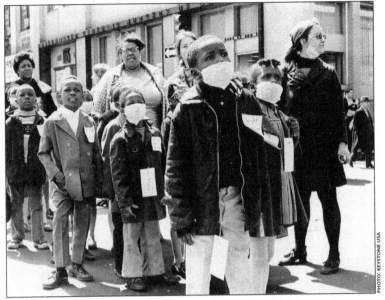

PHOTO: KEYSTONE USA

*Children, teachers and parents
protesting in New York City on Earth Day, 1970*

The Clean Air Act and the Clean Water Act of the 1970s were the direct result of the mass environmental movement, which was part of an overall upsurge in protest movements around the country that began with the civil rights movement and continued through the women's, indigenous, anti-war and LGBTQ rights movements. If the ruling class feels their interests are threatened, they will make some concessions within the capitalist framework, and those concessions will be taken back as soon as there is an ebb in the movement and the ruling class feels they can reverse the people's gains.

What is needed for our survival is the complete transformation of the system that takes control of the wealth and resources of society out of the hands of a few and places it under the control of the many. Under socialism, the trillions of dollars from the annual war budget and the nationalization of the banks could be used to decarbonize the energy and production system. The parasitic health care system — the most costly and inadequate in the world — would be replaced by universal health care with many more trained nurses, doctors and preventive care practitioners so that health services are available in every neighborhood. The assets of the billionaire class would be seized and used to rebuild society for the benefit of the people and planet.

Industries that serve no purpose in the new society, like advertising, fossil fuel production, real estate and insurance would be abolished and those workers would be retrained in other fields.

The imperialist foreign policy of the United States that began with the Spanish American War, which brought the United States to a position of global domination, would end. Under socialism, internationalist cooperation would replace competition with other nations and a culture of sharing and conserving resources would be established. As a first step toward an egalitarian world, reparations would be paid to nations that have suffered bombings, occupations, interventions, and economic exploitation and sabotage at the hands of U.S. imperialism.

Under a socialist planned economy — rather than the inefficient and anarchic capitalist free market — resources will be thoughtfully utilized for the good of people and the planet. The workers in each neighborhood, city and region would decide what is needed locally for the people and the climate to prosper long term, within the goals of an internationally centralized framework so that no historically underserved communities would be left behind. Rather than looking only to allocation of resources over the next quarter like capitalists do, workers' councils will look at immediate needs within the framework of a long-term regenerative relationship with the planet.

Socialism has shown in the past a great capacity to overcome immense challenges that other systems fail to address. China's rapid development within decades from a peasant agrarian society plagued by floods and famine to an industrialized powerhouse is directly due to the efficiency of socialist planning. The Soviet Union was the only country in the world to see economic growth during the Great Depression era that devastated the capitalist economies of the world. The reason that China and Russia have a higher level of development and economic independence today compared to other historically colonized nations is a direct result of their legacy of socialism.

Think about your local city or town and how long it takes to get a road repaved or affordable housing built. Under socialism, where the workers determine what is needed and how to make it happen, true progress can occur much more rapidly.

Millions of Venezuelan housing units have been built to provide 'dignified housing for the people.'

Venezuela's socialist government has built nearly 3 million homes since the Great Housing Project began in 2011, benefiting 12 million people who previously had inadequate housing. They plan to construct another 2 million homes by 2025.[2]

Can you imagine that ever happening in the United States? The only construction that happens quickly are luxury units that enrich investors and developers, while the epidemic of homelessness worsens every day.

Despite its turn toward market socialism and the rise of class contradictions, China is still directed by the Communist Party. This is evident in the rapid development of its renewable energy infrastructure that is leaps and bounds ahead of the United States and Europe, despite the hurdles it faces due to the legacy of colonial underdevelopment that it emerged from just 70 years ago. China has a $100 billion domestic annual investment and $32 billion internationally in renewable energy — more than any other nation. Despite an 18-fold economic growth between 1980 and 2010, China's energy consumption only grew five-fold, reflecting a 70 percent decline in energy intensity. China's 13th Five-Year Plan set the goal of further reductions in energy intensity by 15 percent between 2016 and 2020.[3]

Indigenous people protesting in Brazil against the Amazon fires, deforestation and anti-environment policies

Humanity is facing a pressing 12-year deadline to drastically curb emissions as noted in the 2018 U.N. climate report.[4] A rapid shift to a post-carbon economy could happen very quickly under socialism, particularly in the United States and other wealthier countries where there is an abundance of resources and established infrastructure.

There are movements arising globally against "business as usual" demanding comprehensive action on the climate crisis, largely led by indigenous communities and youth, who see they have no future under the current trajectory. Environmental activists on the front lines worldwide face threat and assassination by local military and thugs acting in the interest of extractive industries, and the number rose to over 200 murdered in 2017 alone.[5] The words of Berta Cáceres, indigenous environmental leader from Honduras assassinated in 2016, ring true: "As long as we keep capitalism, our planet won't be saved because it's the complete opposite of life. We need to end capitalism to save the world and humankind."[6]

The time to act is now. □

Appendix

Humankind is at risk

BY FIDEL CASTRO RUÍZ

The following speech was given by the late Cuban president Fidel Castro Ruíz on June 12, 1992 at the Earth Summit in Rio de Janeiro.

AN important biological species — humankind — is at risk of disappearing due to the rapid and progressive elimination of its natural habitat. We are becoming aware of this problem when it is almost too late to prevent it. It must be said that consumer societies are chiefly responsible for this appalling environmental destruction.

They were spawned by the former colonial metropolis. They are the offspring of imperial policies which, in turn, brought forth the backwardness and poverty that have become the scourge for the great majority of humankind.

With only 20 percent of the world's population, they consume two-thirds of all metals and three-fourths of the energy produced worldwide. They have poisoned the seas and the rivers. They have polluted the air. They have weakened and perforated the ozone layer. They have saturated the atmosphere with gases, altering climatic conditions with the catastrophic effects we are already beginning to suffer.

The forests are disappearing. The deserts are expanding. Billions of tons of fertile soil are washed every year into the sea. Numerous species are becoming extinct. Population pressures and poverty lead to desperate efforts to survive, even at the expense of nature. Third World countries, yesterday's colonies and today nations exploited and plundered by an unjust international economic order, cannot be blamed for all this.

The solution cannot be to prevent the development of those who need it the most. Because today, everything that contributes to underdevelopment and poverty is a flagrant rape of the environment.

As a result, tens of millions of men, women and children die every year in the Third World, more than in each of the two world wars.

Unequal trade, protectionism and the foreign debt assault the ecological balance and promote the destruction of the environment. If we want to save humanity from this self-destruction, wealth and available technologies must be distributed better throughout the planet. Less luxury and less waste in a few countries would mean less poverty and hunger in much of the world.

Stop transferring to the Third World lifestyles and consumer habits that ruin the environment. Make human life more rational. Adopt a just international economic order. Use science to achieve sustainable development without pollution. Pay the ecological debt. Eradicate hunger and not humanity.

Now that the supposed threat of communism has disappeared and there is no more pretext to wage cold wars or continue the arms race and military spending, what then is preventing these resources from going immediately to promote Third World development and fight the ecological destruction threatening the planet?

Enough of selfishness. Enough of schemes of domination. Enough of insensitivity, irresponsibility and deceit. Tomorrow will be too late to do what we should have done a long time ago. □

Endnotes

Preface

1. Paul Hawken, *Drawdown: The Most Comprehensive Plan Ever Proposed to Reverse Global Warming* (New York: Penguin Books, 2017), 118.

2. "The 6 Companies That Own (Almost) All Media [INFOGRAPHIC]," WebFX, accessed December 24, 2019, https://www.webfx.com/data/the-6-companies-that-own-almost-all-media/.

3. Tess Riley, "Just 100 Companies Responsible for 71% of Global Emissions, study says," *The Guardian*, July 11, 2017, https://www.theguardian.com/sustainable-business/2017/jul/10/100-fossil-fuel-companies-investors-responsible-71-global-emissions-cdp-study-climate-change.

4. "Monsoon Floods: Death Toll Rises to More Than 660 in South Asia," *Al Jazeera*, July 23, 2019, https://www.aljazeera.com/news/2019/07/monsoon-floods-death-toll-rises-660-south-asia-190723132358895.html.

5. Dahr Jamail, "In Facing Mass Extinction, We Must Allow Ourselves to Grieve," *Truthout*, January 17, 2019, https://truthout.org/articles/in-facing-mass-extinction-we-dont-need-hope-we-need-to-grieve/.

Chapter 1

1. Chris Hawes, "New CO2 capture technology is not the magic bullet against climate change," *GreenBiz*, April 26, 2019, https://www.greenbiz.com/article/new-co2-capture-technology-not-magic-bullet-against-climate-change-0.

2. Whitney Webb, "U.S. Military Is World's Biggest Polluter," *EcoWatch*, May. 15, 2017, https://www.ecowatch.com/military-largest-polluter-2408760609.html.

Chapter 2

1. "Reforestation Most Effective Against Climate Change," *Deccan Chronicle*, July 7, 2019, https://www.deccanchronicle.com/science/science/070719/reforestation-most-effective-against-climate-change.html.

2. Kay Vandette, "Peatlands: Carbon Sinks on the Brink of Becoming Carbon Emitters," *Earth*, November 19, 2018, https://www.earth.com/news/peatlands-carbon-sinks-emit/.

3. George Monbiot, "The Natural World Can Help Save Us from Climate Catastrophe," *The Guardian*, April 3, 2019, https://www.theguardian.com/commentisfree/2019/apr/03/natural-world-climate-catastrophe-rewilding.

4. "Questions and Answers About Palm Oil," Rainforest Rescue, accessed December 24, 2019, https://www.rainforest-rescue.org/topics/palm-oil/questions-and-answers#start.

5. Mike Wehner, "Scientists Shocked by 75 Percent Decline in Flying Insect Numbers," BGR, October 19, 2017, https://bgr.com/2017/10/19/insect-population-study-research-dramatic-decrease-in-biomass/.

6. Russell McLendon, "6 Things to Know About Earth's 6th Mass Extinction," *Mother Nature Network*, July 11, 2017, https://www.mnn.com/earth-matters/animals/blogs/6-things-to-know-about-earths-6th-mass-extinction.

7. "A Timeline of Earth's Average Temperature," *XKCD*, accessed December 24, 2019, https://xkcd.com/1732/.

8. Monbiot, "Climate Catastrophe."

9. Michael Irving, "Welcome to Pleistocene Park: The mammoth plan to recreate an ice age ecosystem in Siberia," *New Atlas*, April 20, 2018, https://newatlas.com/pleistocene-park-mammoth-ecosystem/54257/.

10. Laura H. Kahn, "Deforestation and Emerging Diseases," *Bulletin of the Atomic Scientists*, February 15, 2011, https://thebulletin.org/2011/02/deforestation-and-emerging-diseases/.

11. Paul Stamets, *Mycelium Running: How Mushrooms Can Help Save the World* (Berkeley: Ten Speed Press, 2005), https://en.wikipedia.org/wiki/Mycelium_Running.

12. Jon Luoma, *The Hidden Forest* (Corvallis: Oregon State University Press, 2006), https://www.publishersweekly.com/978-0-8050-1491-4.

13. "Miyawaki Method," *Forest Creators*, accessed December 24, 2019, https://forestcreators.com/miyawaki-method/.

14. Kim Severson, "From Apples to Popcorn, Climate Change Is Altering the Foods America Grows," *The New York Times*, April 30, 2019, https://www.nytimes.com/2019/04/30/dining/farming-climate-change.html.

15. "Green Revolution," Wikipedia, the free encyclopedia, accessed December 24, 2019, https://en.wikipedia.org/wiki/Green_Revolution.

16. "Scarcity vs. Distribution," *A Well-fed World*, accessed December 24, 2019, https://awfw.org/scarcity-vs-distribution/.

17. Rinkesh, "What Is Desertification?" *Conserve Energy Future*, accessed December 24, 2019, https://www.conserve-energy-future.com/causes-effects-solutions-of-desertification.php.

18. Michael A. Gold, "Agroforestry," *Encyclopaedia Britannica*, Jan 06, 2016, https://www.britannica.com/science/agroforestry.

19. Paul Hawken, *Drawdown: The Most Comprehensive Plan Ever Proposed to Reverse Global Warming* (New York: Penguin Books, 2017).

20. Dayana Andrade and Felipe Pasini, "Life in Syntropy," filmed December 2015, https://challenges.openideo.com/challenge/climate-stories/stories/ernst-gotsch-syntropic-agriculture-agroforestry.

21. Fernando Rebello, "Large-scale Syntropic Farming: Results and Challenges," The Research Center for Syntropic Agriculture, August 19, 2019, https://agendagotsch.com/en/large-scale-syntropic-farming-results-and-challenges/.

22. Ernst Götsch, "Differences Between Organic and Syntropic Farming," *AgendaGötsch*, April 24, 2018, https://agendagotsch.com/en/diferencas-entre-a-agricultura-sintropica-e-organica-2/.

23. Fred Magdoff and Chris Williams, *Creating an Ecological Society*, (New York: Monthly Review Press, 2017), 238-44.

Chapter 3

1. "7 Reasons Why the Ocean Is So Important," *theoceanpreneur*, accessed December 26, 2019, https://theoceanpreneur.com/sailgreen/seven-reasons-ocean-important/.

2. Robert McSweeney, "Scientists Solve Ocean 'Carbon sink' Puzzle," CarbonBrief, February 8, 2017, https://www.carbonbrief.org/scientists-solve-ocean-carbon-sink-puzzle.

3. "Corals and Coral Reefs, Smithsonian Institute, April 2018, https:// ocean.si.edu/ocean-life/invertebrates/corals-and-coral-reefs.
4. "Coral Reef Loss May Double Flood Damages Worldwide," *Times of India*, June 13, 2018, https://timesofindia.indiatimes.com/ home/environment/flora-fauna/coral-reef-loss-may-double-flood-damages-worldwide/articleshow/64571505.cms.
5. Dahr Jamail, *The End of Ice* (New York: The New Press, 2019).
6. Ibid.
7. "Great Barrier Reef: Severe Coral Bleaching Hits Two-Thirds of Reef, Aerial Surveys Show," *Australian Broadcasting Corporation*, April 10, 2017, https://www.abc.net.au/news/2017-04-10/great-barrier-reef-severe-coral-bleaching-hits-two-thirds/8429662.
8. "What Is Coral Bleaching," National Ocean Service, last updated November, 13, 2019, https://oceanservice.noaa.gov/facts/ coral_bleach.html.
9. Damien Cave and Justin Gillis, "Building a Better Coral Reef," *The New York Times*, September 20, 2017, https://www.nytimes. com/2017/09/20/climate/coral-great-barrier-reef.html.
10. http://jeb.biologists.org/content/220/7/1192
11. "What Is a Dead Zone?" National Ocean Service, last updated August 2, 2019, https://oceanservice.noaa.gov/facts/deadzone.html.
12. "Information about Sea Turtles: Why Care?" Sea Turtle Conservancy, accessed December 26, 2019, https://conserveturtles.org/information-about-sea-turtles-why-care/.
13. "Marine Permaculture How it Works! Video," Nonprofit Resource Network, accessed December 26, 2019, https://nprnsb.org/event/ reverse-climate-change-with-marine-permaculture-strategies-for-ocean-regeneration-with-dr-brian-von-herzen/.
14. Ibid.
15. "Microplastics in the Arctic and the Alps May Have Blown in on the Wind," *New Scientist*, August 14, 2019, https://www.new-scientist.com/article/2213560-microplastics-in-the-arctic-and-the-alps-may-have-blown-in-on-the-wind/.
16. Paul Hawken, *Drawdown: The Most Comprehensive Plan Ever Proposed to Reverse Global Warming* (New York: Penguin Books, 2017).
17. Susan Smillie, "From sea to Plate: How Plastic got into our Fish,"

The Guardian, February 14, 2017, https://www.theguardian.com/lifeandstyle/2017/feb/14/sea-to-plate-plastic-got-into-fish.

18. Simon Butler, "Barry Commoner: scientist, activist, radical ecologist," *Green Left*, Oct. 4, 2012, https://www.greenleft.org.au/content/barry-commoner-scientist-activist-radical-ecologist.

19. "The Largest Cleanup in History," The Ocean Cleanup, accessed December 26, 2019, https://www.theoceancleanup.com/, https://www.youtube.com/watch?v=O1EAeNdTFHU.

20. Magdoff and Williams, *Creating an Ecological Society*, 238-39.

Chapter 4

1. https://www.newsweek.com/climate-change-global-warming-ocean-currents-885237.

2. Dahr Jamail, *The End of Ice* (New York: The New Press, 2019).

3. "Climate Change and Vector-Borne Disease," UCAR Center for Science Education, accessed December 28, 2019, https://scied.ucar.edu/longcontent/climate-change-and-vector-borne-disease.

4. Henry Fountain and Nadja Popovich, "March Temperatures in Alaska: 20 Degrees Hotter Than Usual," *The New York Times*, April 9, 2019, https://www.nytimes.com/interactive/2019/04/09/climate/alaska-abnormally-hot-march.html.

5. Julia O'Malley, "Alaska Relies on Ice. What Happens When It Can't Be Trusted?" *The New York Times*, April 10, 2019, https://www.nytimes.com/2019/04/10/us/alaska-ice-melting.html.

6. Jason Samenow, "It was 84 degrees near the Arctic Ocean This Weekend as Carbon dioxide Hit Its Highest Level in Human History," *The Washington Post*, May 14, 2019, https://www.sfgate.com/news/article/It-was-84-degrees-near-the-Arctic-Ocean-this-13843781.php.

7. Ryan W. Miller and Doyle Rice, "Carbon dioxide Levels Hit Landmark at 415 ppm, Highest in Human History," *USA TODAY*, Update May 14, 2019, https://www.usatoday.com/story/news/world/2019/05/13/climate-change-co-2-levels-hit-415-parts-per-million-human-first/1186417001/.

8. Pakalolo, "Arctic Permafrost Thaw Is Awakening the 'Sleeping Giant' of the World's Vast Greenhouse Gas Stores," KOS, December 23, 2018, https://www.dailykos.com/sto-

ries/2018/12/23/1821190/-Arctic-permafrost-thaw-is-lea-ding-to-increased-Ocean-Acidification.

9. Robert Hunz, "Methane SOS," *CounterPunch*," October 11, 2019, https://www.counterpunch.org/2019/10/11/methane-sos.

10. Jamail, *End of Ice*.

11. Damian Carrington, " 'Extraordinary thinning' of ice sheets revealed deep inside Antarctica," *The Guardian*, May 16, 2019, https://www.theguardian.com/environment/2019/may/16/thin-ning-of-antarctic-ice-sheets-spreading-inland-rapidly-study.

12. Jamail, *End of Ice*.

13. Surging Seas, San Francisco Bay Area map, accessed January 1, 2020, https://ss2.climatecentral.org/#15/37.7686/-122.3984?-show = satellite&projections = 0-K14_RCP85-SLR&level = 5&unit = feet&pois = hide.

14. San Francisco Bay Shoreline: Adaptation Atlas, San Francisco Estuary Institute, April 2019, https://www.sfei.org/sites/default/files/toolbox/SFEI%20SF%20Bay%20Shoreline%20Adaptation%20Atlas%20April%202019_lowres.pdf.

15. Peter Fimrite, "Blueprint to Battle Bay Area Sea-level Rise Focuses on Natural Solutions," *San Francisco Chronicle*, May 2, 2019, https://www.sfchronicle.com/science/article/Blueprint-to-battle-Bay-Area-sea-level-rise-13811885.php.

16. "Fukushima Daiichi nuclear disaster," Wikipedia, the free ency-clopedia, accessed January 1, 2020, https://en.m.wikipedia.org/wiki/Fukushima_Daiichi_nuclear_disaster.

17. Leonard Castañeda, "Which Bay Area Companies Didn't Pay Federal Income Taxes in 2018," *Mercury News*, updated April 16, 2019, https://www.mercurynews.com/2019/04/15/which-bay-ar-ea-companies-didnt-pay-federal-income-taxes-in-2018-report/.

18. T.J. Blackman, "The Ecological Benefits of Forest Fires," Eartheasy, September 3, 2015, https://learn.eartheasy.com/arti-cles/the-ecological-benefits-of-forest-fires/. https://www.ucsusa.org/global-warming/science-and-impacts/impacts/infograph-ic-wildfires-climate-change.html.

19. Jonathan Amos, "Arctic wildfires: How Bad Are They and What Caused Them?" *BBC News*, August 2, 2019, https://www.bbc.com/news/world-europe-49125391.

20. "Is Global Warming Fueling Increased Wildfire Risks?" Union of

Concerned Scientists, updated Jul 24, 2018, https://www.ucsusa.org/global-warming/science-and-impacts/impacts/global-warming-and-wildfire.html.

21. David Klein, "100% Renewable Energy: Mark Jacobson Sues for Knowingly False Statements," System Change, not Climate Change, November 25, 2017, https://scncc.net/threads/100-renewable-energy-mark-jacobson-sues-for-knowingly-false-statements.214/.

22. Steve Hanley, "New Mark Z. Jacobson Study Draws a Roadmap to 100% Renewable Energy," CleanTechnica, February 8, 2018, https://cleantechnica.com/2018/02/08/new-jacobson-study-draws-road-map-100-renewable-energy/.

23. Hawken, *Drawdown*.

24. Jamail, *End of Ice*.

25. "In Solar Power Lies Path to Reducing Water Use For Energy," Circle of Blue, August 31, 2010, https://www.circleofblue.org/2010/world/in-solar-power-lies-path-to-reducing-water-use-for-energy/.

26. Hawken, *Drawdown*.

27. Hawken, *Drawdown*.

28. Mohammed Asaduzzaman, Abul Kalam Enamul Haque, Shahidur R. Khandker, Zubair K.M. Sadeque, Hussain A. Samad, Mohammad Yunus, "Surge in Solar-powered Homes : Experience in Off-grid Rural Bangladesh (English)," The World Bank, October 8, 2014, http://documents.worldbank.org/curated/en/871301468201262369/pdf/.

29. "Climate Change and why Nuclear Power Can't Fix it," *Beyond Nuclear*, accessed December 25, 2019, http://static1.1.sqspcdn.com/static/f/356082/28075941/1549560021453/Flyer_ClimateChange_UK.pdf.

30. John Funk, "Ohio bill Would Create 'Clean Air' Fund to Benefit Nuclear, Excluding Wind and Solar," *Energy News Network*, April 5, 2019, https://energynews.us/2019/04/05/midwest/ohio-bill-would-create-clean-air-fund-to-benefit-nuclear-excluding-wind-and-solar/.

31. "Smokescreen Animation - Green New Deal #GND," Fairewinds Energy Education, November 16, 2016, https://www.fairewinds.org/nuclear-energy-education/smokescreen.

Chapter 5

1. "The Story of Stuff," filmed November 2007, video, 18:30, https://storyofstuff.org/movies/story-of-stuff/.
2. Alana Semuels, "Is This the End of Recycling?" *The Atlantic*, March 5, 2019, https://www.theatlantic.com/technology/archive/2019/03/china-has-stopped-accepting-our-trash/584131/.
3. McDonough and Braungart, *The Upcycle* (New York: Melcher Media, 2013).
4. Fred Magdoff and Chris Williams, *Creating an Ecological Society*, (New York: Monthly Review Press, 2017).
5. Mint Press News, "U.S. Military Is World's Biggest Polluter," *EcoWatch*, May 15, 2017, https://www.ecowatch.com/military-largest-polluter-2408760609.html.
6. Lauren Walker, "US military Burn pits Built on Chemical Weapons Facilities Tied to Soldiers' Illness," *The Guardian*, updated on September 20, 2017, https://www.theguardian.com/us-news/2016/feb/16/us-military-burn-pits-chemical-weapons-cancer-illness-iraq-afghanistan-veterans.
7. "Country Overshoot Days," Earth Overshoot Day, accessed January 1, 2020, https://www.overshootday.org/newsroom/country-overshoot-days/.
8. Christopher Jones, Daniel M. M. Kammen, "A Consumption-Based Greenhouse Gas Inventory of San Francisco Bay Area Neighborhoods, Cities and Counties: Prioritizing Climate Action for Different Locations," (UC Berkeley, 2015), https://escholarship.org/uc/item/2sn7m83z.

Chapter 6

1. Paul Hawken, *Drawdown: The Most Comprehensive Plan Ever Proposed to Reverse Global Warming* (New York: Penguin Books, 2017).
2. "La Revolución Energetica: Cuba's Energy Revolution," Renewable Energy World, April 9, 2009, https://www.renewableenergyworld.com/articles/print/volume-12/issue-2/solar-energy/la-revolucion-energetica-cubas-energy-revolution.html.
3. Hawken, *Drawdown*, 102-3.
4. Richard Schiffman, "Mushrooms Are the New Styrofoam," *New*

Scientist, June 12, 2013, https://www.newscientist.com/article/mg21829210-300-mushrooms-are-the-new-styrofoam/.

5. William Schneider, "The Suburban Century Begins," *The Atlantic*, July 1992, https://www.theatlantic.com/past/docs/politics/ecbig/schnsub.htm.

6. "Rent trend data in San Francisco, California," Rent Jungle, accessed January 1, 2020, https://www.rentjungle.com/average-rent-in-san-francisco-rent-trends/.

7. "HUD: $117,000 Now 'Low-Income' In 3 Bay Area Counties," *CBS News San Francisco*, June 26, 2018, https://sanfrancisco.cbslocal.com/2018/06/26/hud-117000-low-income-san-mateo-san-francisco-marin/.

8. "Greenhouse Gas Inventory Data Explorer," U.S. Environmental Protection Agency, accessed January 1, 2020, https://cfpub.epa.gov/ghgdata/inventoryexplorer/.

9. "Annual Report: Protecting Our Community," Bay Area Air Quality Management Board, http://annualreport.baaqmd.gov/2018/protecting-our-community.html.

10. Adele Peters, "See Just How Much of a City's Land Is Used for Parking Spaces," Fast Company, July 20, 2017, https://www.fastcompany.com/40441392/see-just-how-much-of-a-citys-land-is-used-for-parking-spaces.

11. "Climate Change Indicators: Heat-Related Deaths," U.S. Environmental Protection Agency, updated 2016, https://www.epa.gov/climate-indicators/climate-change-indicators-heat-related-deaths.

12. Ian Johnston, "Urban 'Heat Island' Effect Could Intensify Climate Change, Making Cities Up to 7C Warmer, *Independent*, May 29, 2017, https://www.independent.co.uk/environment/urban-heat-island-cities-climate-change-worse-global-warming-7-degrees-cool-roofs-pavements-a7761846.html.

13. *National Geographic Magazine*, April 2019.

14. Alan LaFrance, "Latest Landscaping Industry Statistics and Data for 2019," January 14, 2019, https://www.lawnstarter.com/blog/statistics/latest-landscaping-industry-statistics-and-data-for-2019/.

15. "Lawns in the United States," Wikipedia, the free encyclopedia, accessed January 1, 2020, https://en.wikipedia.org/wiki/Lawns_in_the_United_States.

Chapter 7

1. Fred Magdoff and John Bellamy Foster, What Every Environmentalist Needs to Know About Capitalism (New York: Monthly Review Press, 2011).

2. "'Great Housing Project' Has Benefited 12 Million Venezuelans," *Telesur*, April 16, 2019, https://www.telesurenglish.net/news/Great-Housing-Project-Has-Benefited-12-Million-Venezuelans-20190416-0015.html.

3. Jiang Kejun, "How China is Leading the Renewable Energy Revolution," World Economic Forum, August 29, 2017, https://www.weforum.org/agenda/2017/08/how-china-is-leading-the-renewable-energy-revolution.

4. Umair Irfan, "Report: We Have Just 12 years to Limit Devastating Global Warming," *Vox*, October 8, 2018, https://www.vox.com/2018/10/8/17948832/climate-change-global-warming-un-ipcc-report.

5. Lorraine Chow, "A Record 207 Environmental Activists Were Killed Last Year," *Ecowatch*, July 25, 2018, https://www.ecowatch.com/environmental-activists-killed-2589828107.html.

6. "Berta Cáceres," *Telesur*, accessed January 1, 2020, https://scontent-sjc3-1.xx.fbcdn.net/v/t1.0-9/14333099_-918274988315904_8219306648266775126_n.png?_nc_cat=110&_nc_oc=AQlJ4hxW7BK-n02dudkKSQux-ZpUnelpcjL7CyeRP-mZbTJXxMzG86f0e_R81_GF6rRIXU_Zx2Ez4vfKSJLfdF1ja&_nc_ht=scontent-sjc3-1.xx&oh=54105abcd5a903d6d383e2f93c-5ba7b5&oe=5E24D0C2.